COCAINE

A DRUG
AND ITS SOCIAL
EVOLUTION

Lester Grinspoon
&
James B. Bakalar

Basic Books, Inc., Publishers

NEW YORK

The authors gratefully acknowledge permission to reprint excerpts from the following sources:

"Casey Jones," words by Robert Hunter, © 1970 Ice Nine Publishing Company.

"Earth Mother," © 1971 Steel Wind Publishing Company.

"Let It Bleed," © 1970 ABKCO Music, Inc.

Peru: History of Coca, W. Golden Mortimer, © And/Or Press.

"Sister Morphine," Mick Jagger and Keith Richard, ©1969 ABKCO Music, Inc. All Rights Reserved. International Copyright Secured.

"Snow Blind Friend," words and music by Hoyt Axton, © 1968, Lady Jane Music.

"Take a Whiff on Me," words and music by Huddie Ledbetter, collected and adapted by John A. Lomax and Alan Lomax. TRO— © copyright 1936 and renewed 1964 Folkways Music Publishers, Inc., New York, New York.

Library of Congress Cataloging in Publication Data

Grinspoon, Lester, 1928–
    Cocaine: a drug and its social evolution.

    Bibliography: p. 287
    Includes index.
    1. Cocaine. I. Bakalar, James B., 1943– joint
author. II. Title.
HV5810.G73   362.2'93   76-7675
ISBN: 0-465-01189-6

To our families

CONTENTS

PART III

PREFACE

THIS BOOK is addressed mainly to the nonspecialist but includes a few sections, especially the material on neurophysiology and pharmacology in Chapter 4, that are necessarily somewhat technical. These passages are designed to be comprehensible to those without extensive specialized training, and they are sometimes helpful for an understanding of other sections of the book. Nevertheless, to readers who may find them tedious we offer our apologies and the suggestion that they skim; we believe that they will find the book useful even without them.

There is no objective language for psychoactive drug experiences, and the choice of terminology often implies a moral or social attitude. In the case of cocaine, recent reports in clinical or experimental language are scarce, so it is especially important to take note of the perceptions of the drug users themselves as expressed in their own words. We conducted interviews with 17 people who had at one time used cocaine regularly or were using it at the time of the interview. We obtained subjects by asking several people whom we knew to be familiar with cocaine to refer us to acquaintances who also used it, and then repeated the request with these new subjects. Most of the cocaine users shared their knowledge and opinions with us freely; a few were paid. The subjects ranged in age from 22 to 38; 12 were men and 5 women; 14 were white and 3 black; occupations included student, housewife, receptionist, drug rehabilitation counselor, consultant on urban affairs, radio news reporter, and shop proprietor; some had used cocaine for many years, others had used it intensively for a few months, and still others used it intermittently, when they were able to obtain it; several had given it up for financial or other reasons. Most of the subjects had only sniffed cocaine, but some, including a former heroin addict, had taken it by intravenous injection. The interviews, although lengthy and open-ended, were planned to touch on certain listed topics. We asked about amount and frequency of use, price, quality, the nature of the high, long-term effects, adverse physiological and psychological reactions, sexual effects, tolerance, dependence, withdrawal reactions, comparisons with other drugs, and drug preference. We also tried to find out something about cocaine's effect on the lives of its users by asking them whether most of their friends also used it, whether they took it alone or in company, and whether they thought it had changed their lives for better or for worse. Quotations from these interviews are interspersed throughout the book. We are not suggesting that our subjects are a representative sample or that their remarks cover the full range of experiences associated with cocaine; instead we mean to convey some of the flavor, atmosphere, and language of cocaine use in America today.

For similar reasons we have occasionally used passages from novels and short stories to suggest or confirm the existence of one or another cocaine effect; these quotations are introduced when it seems clear that the author is either describing his own experience in fictional form or has otherwise had a first-hand acquaintance with the drug or its users. Passages of this kind from fiction are not less valuable to a student of cocaine than memoirs or remarks made in interviews; if the writer has some literary talent, they may be more valuable.

We are indebted to a number of people for help in our work. William von Eggers Doering and Norman E. Zinberg read the manuscript and offered critical suggestions. Richard E. Schultes and Andrew Weil gave us the benefit of their experience and knowledge of coca; we are particularly indebted to Dr. Weil for several observations quoted in the book. Timothy Plowman and Charles Sheviak of the Harvard Botanical Museum were kind enough to offer some suggestions for the section on botany and cultivation and provide information on the taxonomy of the coca plant. We also owe thanks to Elizabeth Weiss, Anne C. Bauer, Susan Wolf, and Ogie Strogatz, and a special debt of gratitude to Betsy Grinspoon and Hazel E. Cherney for their invaluable help in preparing the manuscript.

COCAINE

INTRODUCTION

THE STIMULANT and euphoriant extracted from the leaves of the coca plant is becoming one of the most prized, if not most often used, of pleasure-giving drugs. Reports of the arrest of drug smugglers more and more often mention cocaine as their cargo. It is being sniffed or injected more and more openly and frequently by those who can afford it as well as those who have to beg, borrow, steal, or deal to obtain it. Movies and popular songs have-celebrated it or condemned it or done both at once. Articles in national magazines have described its pleasures and warned about its dangers, producing the usual combination of attitudes toward newly popular drugs in which interest predominates over fear. Cocaine has begun to reach the college campuses, where, notoriously, the merely fashionable is admitted into the company of the *Zeitgeist*.

In spite of the growing interest in the drug and its long history in both South America and the United States, ignorance and misapprehensions about it are substantial on both the popular and the scientific levels. Some people confuse the coca leaf with the cacao bean and assume vaguely that cocaine is related to chocolate; others confuse the coca plant with the coconut. A more serious misconception identifies cocaine with opiates; this confusion has been enshrined in laws that are only now first being challenged in the courts. There are also those who still believe that cocaine is a variant of heroin or similar to heroin in its effects, although in actuality the characteristic pleasures and dangers of cocaine and those of morphine or heroin are quite different. On the scientific level information is also surprisingly limited, and very little of it is recent. The most extensive work on the botany, ethnography, and medicinal uses of the coca leaf was published in 1901; the most important medical and psychiatric studies of cocaine abuse were made in the 1920s; most of the work on the effects of coca-leaf chewing on mood and behavior was done in the 1940s. The clinical literature on the effects of cocaine in man remains comparatively sparse, and most of it is over 50 years old. Controlled experimental studies on human beings are almost entirely lacking. The National Institute on Drug Abuse is funding several research projects, and in a few years considerably more will be known. Meanwhile we have to piece together information and conclusions from old case histories, animal experimentation, interviews, literary descriptions, and analogies with the effects of other drugs, especially the much more extensively studied amphetamines.

There are many reasons for taking an interest in cocaine, and no book can satisfy all the different kinds of concerns equally. One is a trivial but harmless curiosity on the level of gossip: a desire to know about the secret practices of the rich, or entertainers, or racial minorities, or adolescents. This can be disguised by or converted to a sociological interest in who takes the drug, when, why, how, and how much, and its connections with other social practices and conditions. Another kind of curiosity is the desire to find out what a drug might do for or to oneself. A false impersonality or objectivity, a pretense of addressing only students who are interested in a problem that is located at a respectable distance from their own lives, may conceal the fact that readers are using a book in this way. On the other hand, many studies openly choose potential drug users or those who are trying to cope with the consequences of drug abuse as their main audience and aim largely to promote or prevent the use of a given drug. Most of the works in the literature on cocaine are of this kind—perhaps unfortunately, since certain facts are selectively overemphasized for polemical purposes. All these matters are secondary to us, although we have included information that is relevant to them.

This book is divided into three parts. The first is a historical and sociological sketch of the use of the coca leaf and cocaine; the second is a description of what is known of the source, pharmacology, and physiological and psychological effects of the drug, including its medical uses; the third is a more general discussion of the problem of drug abuse and the roots of contemporary confusion about psychoactive drugs, with specific reference to the lessons that can be learned from the history of coca and cocaine. We are interested in cocaine primarily as a case study in the cultural definitions of psychoactive drug use. Since cocaine becomes more a subject of open controversy as it becomes more popular, the implications

of this case for public policy are important. In its long history as a medicine, stimulant, and intoxicant, cocaine has been classified in many different ways by different societies and in different eras. This history provides suggestions about the meaning of drug use in several different
social contexts: primitive and archaic ritual and medicine, the labor of the
poor in colonial empires and underdeveloped countries, and industrial society in a period when attitudes toward drugs and drug technology were
undergoing a revolutionary change. The nineteenth-century developments that fixed our present established attitudes toward cocaine are
especially interesting. By examining them we can suggest some reasons
why nonmedical use of psychoactive drugs generates such strong pas-
sions and controversial public policies in our society. Present attitudes
toward cocaine as well as other drugs that affect the mind may change as
the historical conditions that created them disappear.

Our interest in the historical aspect of public policy on cocaine is insep-
arable from a concern about what that policy should be in the future, and
more generally about the intellectual and moral basis of all public controls on psychoactive drugs. Therefore we have restated the general problem of drug dependence and drug abuse as applied to the particular case
of cocaine. Cocaine is sometimes referred to as a drug problem or even as
part of *"the* drug problem." Although the concern these phrases express
is admirable, they are misleading. They tend to make us overemphasize
the question of what we should do about "it" (the drug) or, worse, about
"them" (the drug users), with unpleasant overtones of condescension,
envy, or scapegoating. Instead we should be asking what to do about ourselves and our society. Although that question may seem too general to be
meaningful, it saves us from the kind of premature definition and classification of problems that has been so disastrous in our treatment of the
use of psychoactive substances. A redefinition of our ideas about these
drugs has begun in recent years, first among the general public and now
among physicians; it has produced more careful differentiations and at
the same time more flexibility and tolerance of ambiguity. We hope this
study of cocaine will contribute to that process. Although the use of drugs
in general and cocaine in particular may not be in itself as important a
social issue as the attention devoted to it sometimes suggests, the amount
and quality of the interest in this subject is significant as a symptom of
present social conditions and an indication for the future. By lifting some
of the fog surrounding the cocaine issue, and especially by clarifying its
historical aspects and its relation to general problems of drug dependence
and drug abuse, we hope to promote the kind of rational public decision

that has been rare where psychoactive drugs are concerned. The emotional obstacles to considering these substances calmly and in a large enough context are great, but the effort is worth making. For the questions discussed (almost always inadequately and with the wrong focus) under the rubric of drug problems involve, at their broadest extent, the kind of society and the kind of humanity we want and are capable of creating.

PART I

THE COCA LEAF

THE PLANT from which cocaine is extracted has been cultivated in South America for thousands of years, and a large part of the population of Bolivia and Peru, smaller numbers in Colombia, and a few people in Argentina and Brazil, now chew its leaf every day. One student of the coca leaf has gone so far as to write of the Peruvian Indians, "Never in the life of a people has a plant had such importance." [1] A sixteenth-century Spanish administrator of the conquered Inca empire said, "If there were no coca, there would be no Peru." [2] The magical leaf that, in the words of the early chronicler Garcilaso de la Vega (himself of Inca and Spanish descent and the heir to a coca plantation), "satisfies the hungry, gives new strength to the weary and exhausted and makes the unhappy forget their sorrows" became perhaps even more important when the Spanish conquest made its consumption more widespread. Since then it has been alternately extolled and condemned, and it remains a topic of controversy today.

No one knows where *Erythroxylum coca* first grew wild or was first used as a drug: the present wild varieties are the descendants of once-cultivated plants in abandoned fields, and coca use may have begun in one region or in several different areas at different times. It has been suggested that coca chewing originated among the Arhuacos of the Rio Negro area or in the central Amazon. The Aymara Indians in Bolivia apparently used it before the Inca conquest (tenth century A.D.), and the word *coca* itself is thought to be of Aymara origin; it means simply "plant" or "tree," which suggests that coca was regarded as *the* plant, the plant of plants. Statues found in graves on the coast of Peru and Ecuador dated at about 300 B.C. sometimes have the puffed-out cheeks that indicate a wad of coca in the mouth. The drug was once used in northern South America from the Venezuela coast to the region of Arica in Chile, and also on the Pacific coast of Nicaragua and the Caribbean coast of Panama. Its Caribbean name was *hayo*. Although coca use has declined or disappeared over much of its former range, many tribes in the Amazon basin and in the Colombian mountains still use it. But at least since the time of the Incas the center of coca cultivation has been the warm valleys on the eastern slopes of the Andes, and the center of coca chewing has been the highlands of Bolivia and Peru.[3]

Under the Incas coca had sacred status. It was used in divination and scattered by priests before religious rites to propitiate the gods. The mouth of a corpse might be filled with coca and bags of the leaves deposited in the tomb to ease the journey to the next world. It was incorporated in amulets used to attain riches or success in love and played an important part in weddings, funerals, and the *huaraca,* or initiation rite for young Inca nobles. Each useful plant was thought to have a divine essence, its "mother." There were "mothers" of maize, quinine, and coca— Mama Coca, sometimes pictured as a beautiful woman, with associated myths. One of the Inca rulers gave his queen the title Mama Coca. Precisely because of its high status, the actual use of coca among the populace was very restricted. The early chroniclers almost all affirm that it was rarely available to the common people before the Spanish conquest. The Inca elite controlled most cultivation in state-owned *cocales* or coca plantations and permitted its use only in religious rites and as a special royal gift. Although the masses used coca ceremonially and as a medicine, it was not, as it is now, the daily drug of millions.[4]

The first impulses of the conquerors were hostile to coca. In some regions, like the Pacific coast of Peru, *cocales* were in fact abandoned, and the use of the drug declined. At ecclesiastical councils in 1551 and 1567 the bishops of the Catholic church formally denounced its use as idolatry, and a royal proclamation declared its effects a demoniacal illusion. But by that time Spaniards were already putting it to use in the silver and gold mines and on the plantations, and growing rich from the trade in it. The church eventually found it possible to condone the cultivation of coca while outlawing its religious use: taxes on coca actually provided the sixteenth-century bishops and canons of Cuzco with much of their revenue. A royal order under the Viceroy Francisco de Toledo in 1573 in effect removed official obstacles to the cultivation of the coca plant. The inclusion of its leaf after the Wars of Independence in the coat-of-arms of Peru as a symbol of endurance constitutes both a gesture toward its former status and a recognition of its present importance.[5]

Why did the use of coca become so much more widespread in the highlands after the Spanish conquest? One apparent cause is the breakdown of the religious restrictions imposed by the Incas. Another possible reason is the havoc wrought by the conquerors on the food economy— much fruit and grain cultivation was abandoned and the livestock industry was destroyed.[6] Coca is often chewed most in regions where the diet is poorest: the drug that "satisfies the hungry" serves as a substitute for food. But no historical analysis has yet explained why coca survived where it did and not elsewhere; for example, the use of the coca leaf has been almost extinct since the eighteenth century in the highlands of northern Peru and Ecuador, areas that are climatically, culturally, and historically similar to some of the regions where it is chewed daily.

The liberation of South America from Spanish colonial rule did not change the conditions of Indian life or the practice of coca chewing. In 1850, for example, 8 percent of the revenue of the government of Bolivia came from the coca trade. In the three centuries before its introduction into western Europe, most Peruvians and Bolivians were complacent about coca and few regarded it as a drug problem or as any kind of problem. In 1787 the Jesuit priest Antonio de Julián suggested that it be permanently substituted for tea and tobacco; the most famous Peruvian physician of the eighteenth century, Hipólito Unánue, praised its stimulant effect and other medicinal virtues. The discovery of the surgical uses of cocaine in 1884 and its vogue in late nineteenth-century Europe and the United States even induced a kind of patriotic pride.[7]

In the twentieth century, cultivation of coca has continued at the same level, while controversy about it has become sharper. Newly conscious of the poverty and misery of the Indians, and observing the consequences of cocaine abuse in Europe and North America, Peruvian and Bolivian physicians have begun to reexamine the question of coca chewing. At least since 1929, when Dr. Carlos A. Ricketts presented a plan for the reduction of coca cultivation to the Peruvian parliament, opposition to the drug has been growing. But public opinion has not followed physicians in their nearly unanimous rejection of coca. In 1947 Drs. Carlos Gutiérrez-Noriega and Vicente Zapata Ortiz could still write, "Cocaism, in a word, is not recognized as a public health problem." [8] Official publicity about real or imagined dangers of the drug and efforts at restriction of its use over the last 25 years attest that this is no longer true. But the rural population of Bolivia and Peru has not acquiesced in the official definition of coca use as a health problem, which is enforced halfheartedly by law and not at all by custom.

The issue of coca's possible harmfulness and what ought to be done about it is complicated by the fact that important and legally respected economic and political interests are at stake, as in the case of alcohol and tobacco in this country. Gutiérrez-Noriega, who attacked planters and businessmen for making their fortunes from the misery of the Indians, was dismissed from his post at the University of Lima in 1948 and went into exile; the Institute of Pharmacology he founded was dissolved. The Tax Collection Department of the Coca Monopoly in Peru reported in 1962 that eradication of the coca habit would put 200,000 people out of work. Coca plants may be cultivated in preference to other crops because they are hardier and therefore economically safer. Besides, the coca trade provides regional economic integration and participation in a cash economy. One study of coca chewing in southern Peru indicates that upper-class plantation owners, *mestizo* merchants, and small Indian farmers are united in their opposition to any attempt to eradicate the use of the drug. It is hardly surprising that to many people in Peru and Bolivia dislike of coca has some of the crankish aspect of prohibitionism.[9]

The difficulty of changing such attitudes—whether they need to be changed is another matter—is suggested by the struggle of the UN and its international drug control machinery to make the governments of Peru and Bolivia do something about coca. A United Nations Commission of Enquiry visited those countries in 1950 and concluded that coca chewing "leads to genuinely harmful, closely related economic and social effects in both Peru and Bolivia." It recommended a 15-year program of gradual reduction in cultivation and use. A Peruvian Commission for the Study of the Coca Problem was then formed and challenged the methods and conclusions of the UN study. Dr. Carlos Monge, a student of high-altitude biology and former Surgeon General of the Peruvian army, defended the position of this commission, which was also the position of the Peruvian government, at a United Nations meeting in December 1950, and the UN commission responded.[10]

Since then the governments of Bolivia and Peru have formally relinquished their dissenting opinion, ratifying the measures proposed by the UN without doing much about putting them into effect. The Single Convention on Narcotic Drugs of 1961 was signed by Peru and approved by Bolivia: it required the abolition of coca-leaf chewing and the destruction of most coca bushes within 25 years. It is unlikely that this will happen. Commissions and consultative groups and regional meetings under the auspices of the UN continue to advocate abolition or at least that the

conditions for abolition be created by providing substitute crops and occupations and other sources of tax revenue. Government information
campaigns and various restrictions and registration requirements have
been instituted. But official figures on coca production are probably as
unreliable as official figures on whiskey production in Kentucky, and the
recent increase in the number of illicit cocaine factories servicing the international trade will make them even more unreliable. The state institu-
tion known as the Coca Monopoly in Peru probably has less control over
the coca market than General Motors has over the automobile market in
the United States. The International Narcotics Control Board of the UN
admits that very little has changed since it began its campaign against
the coca leaf in 1950.[11]

Various estimates of the total production and consumption of coca are
available. The United Nations Commission of Enquiry asserted in 1950
that about half the rural adult population of Peru and Bolivia—a quarter
of the total adult population—chewed the coca leaf. It was said to be used
mostly by men; only 20 percent of the women chewed it.[12] A 1965 study
indicated that 13 percent of the people of Peru, more than half the working rural population, used coca. Fifty-seven percent of the *coqueros*, or
coca chewers, were men and 43 percent were women. By extrapolation it
has been estimated that in 1970, 1,165,000 Peruvians out of 11,000,000
were using the drug. It is, overwhelmingly, a lower-class habit. Sixty percent of Peruvian *coqueros*, according to the 1965 study, are illiterate, as
opposed to 18.5 percent of nonusers; only 0.2 percent of users have any
secondary education, as opposed to 22 percent of nonusers. Twenty-nine
percent of coca chewers are farm workers, 25 percent housewives, 8.5
percent domestic servants, and 8.4 percent artisans. Official Peruvian agricultural statistics for 1971 show a production of 14,351,000 kg, only a
small proportion of which is legally converted into cocaine. Production
has been rising, and although there is some question whether it is keeping pace with population increase, there has apparently not been any
serious decline in coca use.[13]

Although there are remnants of its former cultural status in folk religion and medicine, coca in the Andean highlands is largely an everyday
drug, used mainly at work. The practice varies from place to place and individual to individual and is not exactly the same in mines or factories as
on farms, but coca use is characterized by daily regularity. The agricultural work day, according to the UN commission, lasts from 7:00 A.M. to
5:00 P.M., with three breaks totaling three to four hours for rest and coca
chewing. Emilio Ciuffardi, who made a study of coca use in Peru in 1949,
states that the men in his sample who chewed only on days when they

worked took breaks for this purpose from 9:00 A.M. to 11:00 A.M., from 2:00 P.M. to 4:00 P.M., and from 7:00 P.M. to 9:00 P.M. Those who chewed daily whether they were working or not might take as many as four or five breaks. The Peruvian Coca Monopoly reports that there is a short break at 10:00 A.M. and a longer one at 3:00 P.M. A few men apparently chew continously during their waking hours.[14] One writer has estimated that the Peruvian Indian may devote 25 percent of his income to buying coca; employers since the time of the conquest have sometimes paid wages in coca leaves rather than money. It has been estimated that in the region of Nuñoa, in southern Peru, a day's work for the average Indian provides enough money for a little over a week's supply of coca.[15] The period for which a wad of coca is kept in the mouth, 45 minutes, has become a standard unit of time known as the *cocada*. The *cocada* also serves as a distance measure, since it corresponds to three kilometers of walking with a pack on level ground, or two kilometers uphill.

Coca is used as follows. The leaves, carried in a sack (called in some regions a *chuspa*), are moistened with saliva and then wedged in the back of the mouth between the cheek and the gum, like chewing tobacco, on one or both sides. An alkaline substance known as *tocra* or *llipta,* which usually consists of plant ashes of some kind (the most common is *quínoa*) but may also be powdered seashells or quicklime, is added with a stick from a little flask made out of a gourd and called the *iscupuru* or *poporo.* (It is thought that the purpose of the alkali is to release the alkaloids from the leaf and speed their absorption into the bloodstream.) The alkaloids apparently reach the bloodstream partly through the stomach and small intestine as they trickle into the throat dissolved in saliva, and partly through the mucous membrane of the mouth. The verb "to chew" *(masticar),* although sometimes used in Spanish and always in English, is inaccurate except as applied to the preliminary moistening of the leaves. The process of ingestion, which actually resembles sucking, is usually called *acullicar* to the south, *cacchar* farther north, and *mambear* in Colombia. The only significant variation on this method is the Amazonian practice of toasting and pulverizing the dried leaves and mixing cecropia leaf ashes with the powder before placing it between the cheek and gum. One small tribe adds the resin of a plant of the myrrh family to the coca-ash mixture to give it a balsamic savor.[16]

Whether the coca leaf is chewed in this way or taken in powdered form or as a tea, it fills the role of an all-purpose healing herb, like opium in some regions of southeast Asia or cannabis in Jamaica. It might be said to combine the functions of coffee, tobacco, aspirin, and bicarbonate of soda in our society. The South American Indians anticipated most of the uses for cocaine that became popular in Europe and the United States in the late nineteenth century. Folk-healing practices are not just anthropological curiosities; we discuss Indian uses of coca further in Chapter 7, on the place of cocaine in medicine.

In spite of its everyday character, coca is not yet so completely a profane, secularized drug as coffee or aspirin is for us. The Inca and pre-Inca legends associating it with Mama Quilla (the moon) and other goddesses have not been entirely forgotten, and newer legends ascribe its origin to Jesus and the Virgin Mary. Many social and domestic activities are solemnized by the use of coca. Travelers exchange handfuls of leaves as a greeting. It is chewed at religious festivals (where alcohol is also used) and offered to Pacha Mama, the earth, against bad harvests. Indians used to pray to Mama Coca before starting on a journey, and there was a custom, called *jacho lajay,* of sticking a chewed wad of coca (*jacho*) on a stone to propitiate the gods at dangerous places on mountain paths. Miners used to stick the *jacho* to a hard vein of ore to "soften" it as they chewed the leaf to lighten their own labors.[17] The Indians also have songs about coca, some connected with marriage, with bawdy double meanings; others about the Holy Family and their gift of coca; and still others that are solemn and philosophical songs of praise:

> *Pretty little round-leafed coca*
> *the only one who understands my life. . . .*
> *Curative herb of the highlands*
> *Medicinal herb of the puñas*
> *you who understand man's life*
> *you are the only one who knows my fate.*[18]

The religious beliefs associated with coca have lost much of their power, but this heritage of the Incas is not yet entirely exhausted.

Coca is also used by Indians in certain areas of the Colombian Andes and the Colombian and Brazilian Amazon. For example, the Páez of the western highlands of Colombia, with 30,000 members the largest tribe in that country, have cultivated coca for four centuries. Their way of using it is similar to that of the Peruvians and Bolivians. Most of the people, including many women and children, chew it. When a child has learned how to chew, at about the age of eight, he is considered ready to work. The Páez also employ coca as medicine, in divination, and as a medium of exchange.[19] Smaller and more isolated tribes may have very different social definitions of coca use. A striking example is the Kogi of the Sierra Nevada de Santa Marta, also in Colombia. Among these people the religious role of coca is pervasive. Its use is forbidden to women, who harvest the crop but are not permitted to cultivate it. The initiation ceremo-

nies for young men include a marriage to the coca leaf. The men use coca
in religious ceremonies for mental lucidity and physical vigor. It enables
them to stay awake, to fast, to abstain sexually, and to "speak of the ancestors"—sing, recite, and dance for long periods of time. Kogi priests induce trance by means of a mixture of coca and tobacco (which also has
many religious uses among the Colombian Indians). The men say that it
stimulates sexual desire in the early years and later produces impotence.
Kogi men are said not to value sex highly and not to be much troubled by
impotence. The women regard coca as a rival power and if they are child-
less may try to get their husbands to stop using it.[20]

Andrew Weil describes the everyday use of coca in still another region,
the Amazon basin:

> In 1974 I lived among a group of Cubeo Indians on the Río Cuduyari in eastern
> Colombia near the Brazilian border. These people grew their own coca and
> prepared it in the traditional Amazonian way: they toasted and pulverized the
> leaves and mixed them with *Cecropia* leaf ashes to a fine gray-green powder
> that is placed in the mouth and allowed to dissolve slowly. This is an especially
> powerful preparation of coca, and every family in the village I stayed in had its
> own can of it, available for use at all times. Yet I never saw it used except on
> two kinds of occasions. One was to facilitate physical work. For instance, men
> who went out to chop trees down to prepare a new area for planting crops
> would fortify themselves with large helpings of coca as they marched out of the
> village. The other occasion was a fiesta, where everyone drank freshly made
> beer (*chicha*), played music, and danced. Coca would be passed around at
> these ritualized gatherings, and those who wished could partake. I never saw
> children use it, and adolescents and women generally declined it.[21]

The past and present social functions of coca in South America suggest
the wide variety of possible cultural definitions of drug use. Under the
Incas coca was a semisacred substance employed in rituals, and the Kogi
still use it as a medium of transcendence and communication with
spirits. In Peru and Bolivia today it is mainly a stimulant that eases labor,
although it also remains important in folk medicine. Its derivative, cocaine, a product of modern Western science and industry, has had a different fate; at first it too was considered a medicine and general stimulant, but now its use is almost exclusively recreational. With the
introduction of coca to the United States and Europe, a double transformation took place that made the drug a new one, pharmacologically and
socially: cocaine replaced the coca leaf as the center of interest, and the
use of cocaine ceased to have anything to do with medicine or religion
and came to be defined as an illicit pleasure.

2

EARLY HISTORY OF COCAINE

EUROPEANS began to learn about the coca leaf soon after the discovery of America, but for hundreds of years they had practically no firsthand experience of its effects, and their knowledge had the vagueness and dubiety of legend. Why this is so is not clear. The contrast with tobacco, which immediately spread to the Old World and became important in international trade, is striking. Most writers on this subject believe that coca leaves were not properly packed or cared for and so became inert on the long ocean voyage. Another possibility is that the Spanish were so obsessed with the gold and silver of Peru that, in spite of the importance of coca in the internal economy of their colony, they never seriously considered it as another potential commodity in international trade. It is also true that many of the *conquistadores* considered coca chewing, as well as most other native customs, a vice, and did not want to encourage it among Europeans. In any case, for many years the reports about coca that reached Europe had some of the same air of the fabulous that characterized other tales of the Inca Empire.

The first-generation chroniclers of the Spanish conquest refer to coca with more scorn than interest. For example, Pedro Cieza de León, a traveler and soldier in South America from 1532 to 1550, one of the first writers to describe coca chewing for a European audience, remarked, "When I asked some of these Indians why they carried these leaves in their mouths . . . they replied that it prevents them from feeling hungry, and gives them great vigor and strength. I believe that it has some such effect, although perhaps it is a custom only suitable for people like these Indians." [1] Later comments, however, tended to be enthusiastic. None are more so than the verses of Abraham Cowley, a British physician and poet who celebrated the legendary virtues of coca in 1662 in his *Books of Plants*. He presents a South American goddess speaking to Bacchus and Venus:

> *Behold how thick with leaves it is beset;*
> *Each leaf is fruit, and such substantial fare,*
> *No fruit beside to rival it will dare.*
> *Mov'd with his country's coming fate, whose soil*
> *Must for her treasurers be exposed to spoil,*
> *Our Varicocha first this coca sent,*
> *Endowed with leaves of wondrous nourishment,*
> *Whose juice sucked in, and to the stomach taken*
> *Long hunger and long labor can sustain:*
> *From which our faint and weary bodies find*
> *More succor, more they cheer the drooping mind,*
> *Than can your Bacchus and your Ceres joined.* [2]

Other favorable references to coca appear in the writings of the Peruvian physician Hipólito Unánue, who tells of its use in the siege of La Paz (1774) to help the inhabitants bear the hunger, fatigue, and cold, and in the works of the German scientist and explorer Alexander von Humboldt. [3] The first botanical description of the coca plant appeared in a book by Nicolas Monardes, a Spanish physician, published in 1580 and translated into English in 1582 by John Frampton under the title *Joyfulle News Out of the Newe Founde Worlde, wherein is declared the Virtues of Herbs, Treez, Oyales, Plantes, and Stones.* [4] In 1750 the botanist Joseph de Jussieu sent the first specimens to Europe for examination, and the plant eventually received the classification *Erythroxylon coca* Lamarck. [5]

In the nineteenth century, travelers' reports continued to be overwhelmingly favorable. Observers like Johann Jakob von Tschudi (1846), Clements Markham (1856 and 1862), and H. A. Weddell (1853) were impressed by its power of physical invigoration and its effectiveness in respiratory troubles at high altitudes. Tschudi wrote, "I am clearly of the opinion that moderate use of coca is not merely innocuous, but that it may even be very conducive to health." [6] The praise reached a height in an essay by the neurologist Paolo Mantegazza (1859), which was very influential in the late nineteenth century and had a particularly strong impact on Sigmund Freud. [7] One of the few dissenters was Eduard Poeppig, a German physician who published his travel journals in 1836 and was often quoted by later critics of coca. He thought that the inveterate *coquero* was "the slave of his passion even more than the drunk" and "incapable of pursuing any serious goals in life," and contended that coca chewing caused anemia and various digestive troubles.[8] About his writings William Prescott, the great historian of the conquest of Peru, comments in a footnote: "A traveler [Poeppig] expatiates on the malignant effects of the habitual use of the coca as very similar to those produced on the chewer of opium. Strange that such baneful properties should not be the subject of more frequent comment by other writers! I do not remember to have seen them even adverted to." [9]

At about the time Europe began to know the properties of coca as something more than legend, rumor, and questionable travelers' tales, the leaf's main active principle was isolated. In 1855 Ernst von Bibra published *Die Narkotischen Genussmittel und der Mensch,* which gave accounts of 17 drugs, including coffee, tea, hashish, opium, and coca; in the same year Friedrich Gaedcke (correct spelling—the name is variously spelled in the sources) produced from a distillate of the dry residue of an extract of coca a crystalline sublimate he called "Erythroxylin," which was probably a mixture of alkaloids including cocaine. After further attempts by various chemists, Albert Niemann of Göttingen finally isolated the principal alkaloid in 1860 from Peruvian leaves brought to Europe by a Dr. Scherzer. Wilhelm Lossen ascertained the chemical formula of cocaine in 1862, and later in the nineteenth century researchers completed the isolation and description of the other coca alkaloids. Throughout the late nineteenth century both coca itself (that is, an extract from the leaf including all its alkaloids) and the pure chemical cocaine were used as medicines and for pleasure—the distinction was not always made—in an enormous variety of ways.

We have referred to Mantegazza as one of the most important early sources of the new European interest in coca. He adopted an exaggeratedly lyrical tone that may have aroused some skepticism: "I flew about in the spaces of 77,438 worlds, one more splendid than another. I prefer a life of ten years with coca to one of a hundred thousand without it. It seemed to me that I was separated from the whole world, and I beheld the strangest images, most beautiful in color and in form, that can be imagined." [10] Very few of the physicians who later tried coca on themselves or their patients reported any experience like this. But Mantegazza gave enough detail to convince even so sane and astute a clinician as Freud that coca was a useful medicine.[11] Freud and others were un-

doubtedly reassured of Mantegazza's reliability by some cautionary qualifications in which he ascribed digestive complaints, emaciation, and
"moral depravity" to overuse of the drug. If coca had in fact often produced the extravagant "psychedelic" effects described by Mantegazza,
physicians would have been reminded of opium dreams or alcoholic delirium and the drug would not have become nearly so popular. It made its
reputation as a tonic and analgesic.

At first the popularity of coca and cocaine grew steadily but slowly.
Mantegazza recommended coca in 1859 for toothache, digestive disor-
ders, neurasthenia, and other illnesses. In 1863 Angelo Mariani, a Cor-
sican chemist, patented a preparation of coca extract and wine, "Vin
Mariani," that eventually made his fortune, becoming one of the most
popular prescription medicines of the age. As early as 1865 Dr. Charles
Fauvel of Paris was prescribing Mariani preparations for various complaints, including soreness of the larynx and pharynx. According to
Freud, he called coca "la tenseur par excellence des chordes vocales." [12]
In 1868 Tomas Moreno y Maíz, Surgeon General of the Peruvian army,
experimented with cocaine and said that it gave him "some of the most
blessed moments of my life." Charles Gazeau in 1870 took 20 to 30 grams
of coca leaf a day for two days and found that it suppressed his appetite
completely; he thought the appetite-suppressing and invigorating powers
might have military applications. In 1876 there was a flurry of interest in
the British medical press when several men, including the 78-year-old
Dr. Robert Christison of Edinburgh, reported that coca had enabled them
to walk long distances without food or sleep and with no serious aftaref-
fects. The *British Medical Journal* prophesied in an editorial that coca
would prove to be "a new stimulant and a new narcotic: two forms of novelty in excitement which our modern civilization is highly likely to es-
teem." Three weeks later the *Journal* referred to the use of coca in
France as an elixir and wine and by the week after that was apparently
receiving inquiries which prompted the comment that some ladies hoped
it would give them "strength and beauty forever." The literature was
fairly extensive by the time Bordier reviewed it in the *Dictionnaire en-
cyclopédique des sciences médicales* in 1876 and recommended the use of
coca by armies and in industry. [13]

Through the late 1870s and early 1880s the literature on coca and
cocaine continued to grow. An advertising pamphlet published by
Mariani in 1880 could cite numerous favorable references to coca from
the medical press. By 1878 coca was being recommended in advertisements in the United States for "young persons afflicted with timidity in
society" and as "a powerful nervous excitant." In the same year, fatefully,

W. H. Bentley began to promote it as a cure for morphine addiction.* In
1880 Bentley's article in the Detroit *Therapeutic Gazette,* "Erythroxylon
Coca in the Opium and Alcohol Habits," cited several "cures," including
the case of a rich woman, age 72, who had been using opium for 35 years
and was now alternating two weeks of coca with two weeks of opium (a
combination that, in the stronger form of cocaine and heroin, still has its
attractions). In another *Therapeutic Gazette* article that same year, Bentley called coca "the desideratum . . . in health and disease." He claimed
to have cured a "great rake" of impotence with it and to have used it himself since 1870. The *Gazette,* in an editorial published earlier that year,
breezily quoted a breezy editorial in the *Louisville Medical News:* " 'One
feels like trying coca, with or without the opium-habit. A harmless remedy for the blues is imperial.' And so say we." [14] Medical journals today
rarely use this style or openly promote the identification of pleasure with
cure in this way.

Between 1880 and 1884 the *Therapeutic Gazette* published 16 reports
of cures of the opium habit by coca. By 1883 Parke Davis, the American
manufacturer of cocaine, was advertising it in medical journals for morphinism and alcoholism. (The sharp distinction between coca and cocaine that later became a favorite point with advocates of coca was rarely
made at that time). [15] The fluid extract of coca was admitted to the U.S.
Pharmacopoeia in 1882. In 1883 Aschenbrandt clandestinely put cocaine
into the water of Bavarian soldiers before they went on maneuvers and
obtained the expected results. There were still some skeptics, like George
Ward, a physician who had spent three years in Cerro-del-Pasco, Peru, at
an altitude of 14,000 feet; he doubted that coca had any more effect than
whiskey or tea. [16] But coca and cocaine were about to realize their potential popularity.

The *annus mirabilis* was 1884. Until then, possibly because the diver-
sity of claims about its effects was confusing and possibly because preparations were of unreliable quality, cocaine had not attained the renown

---

* Since we intend to use the word *addiction* in connection with morphine and heroin (diacetylmorphine), we must insist that we do not intend it to carry the misleading emotional connotations it has
acquired because of public hysteria and legal persecution. As we use the term in this book, it is simply a
convenient way of referring to the fact that these drugs sometimes produce severe physiological abstinence symptoms. The same is true of barbiturates and alcohol. Many alcoholics could just as well be
called alcohol addicts. And just as people can drink liquor without becoming alcoholics, they can smoke,
sniff, or inject opiates without becoming addicts. Addiction to opiates occurs earlier in the course of habitual use than addiction to alcohol, but in almost all other ways alcohol addiction is much worse. The abstinence symptoms in alcohol (and barbiturate) addiction are much more severe than in opiate addiction;
unlike opiate abstinence symptoms, they can be fatal without proper medical care. More important, the
potential acute and chronic toxic effects of the *use* of alcohol and barbiturates, as opposed to withdrawal,
are much greater than those of opiate use. We discuss drug addiction and dependence in detail in
Chapter 8.

some thought it deserved. The decisive events were the publication of Freud's paper "On Coca" in July and Karl Koller's rediscovery in September of the anesthetic power of cocaine, which meant the advent of local anesthesia in surgery. Freud's still useful article, written with what Ernest Jones calls "a remarkable combination of objectivity and personal warmth, as though he were in love with the object itself," created a sensation.[17] He reviewed the historical and medical literature and contended that coca (he makes no distinction between coca and cocaine) should be regarded as a stimulant like caffeine and not a narcotic like opium and cannabis. He blamed the drug's past failures on bad quality preparations. On the authority of various physicians and from his own experience he recommended coca or cocaine for a variety of illnesses, and especially for the congeries of symptoms including fatigue, nervousness, and small physical complaints then known as neurasthenia, which he was later to associate with sexual repression. He described the effect of cocaine on himself (apparently taken orally at this time) in doses of 50 to 100 mg as "exhilaration and lasting euphoria, which does not differ in any way from the euphoria of a normal person." He also felt an increase in self-control and vigor without the "characteristic urge for immediate activity which alcohol produces" or the "heightening of the mental powers which alcohol, tea, or coffee induce," and he had the capacity but not the need to sleep or eat. Probably the most significant passage in this paper was his praise of cocaine as a cure for morphine addiction and alcoholism, based on the American reports and on his own observation. He believed that coca directly antagonized the effect of morphine and insisted that treatment with coca did not turn the morphine addict into a *coquero*. (By "coca" here he meant cocaine).[18] It was in reference to the writings of Freud and his friend Ernst von Fleischl-Marxow that the Parke Davis company's pamphlet *Coca Erythroxylon and Its Derivatives* declared: "If these claims are substantiated . . . [cocaine] will indeed be the most important therapeutic discovery of the age, the benefit of which to humanity will be incalculable." [19]

Freud's article was influential, but the discovery of the use of cocaine in surgery by the friend and colleague whose interest in the drug he had aroused was of more permanent importance. It had been known for a long time that cocaine was a local anesthetic. Folk medicine in South America makes use of this property, and skulls have been found on archaeological sites in the Andes with holes indicating that trepanation, possibly with the help of coca's pain-deadening effect, was performed. Samuel Percy read a paper on anesthesia by means of coca to the New York Medical Society in 1857. In 1862 Schroff noted the numbing effect of cocaine on the tongue. By 1865 Fauvel was using coca to soothe sore throats. Moreno y Maíz (1868) and Alexander Bennett (1874) demonstrated its anesthetic effect on the mucous membranes. Von Anrep (1878) also proposed its use as an anesthetic. In 1880 Coupart and Bordereau described anesthesia of the cornea of animals' eyes with cocaine.[20]

But somehow no one thought of the seemingly obvious application to surgery until Koller introduced it as a topical anesthetic in eye operations. He filled a desperate need. General anesthesia was unsatisfactory in ophthalmology because the conscious cooperation of the patient was often necessary and because ether, as then administered, could cause retching and vomiting, which, if they occurred during or soon after surgery, might damage the eye. Delicate, sensitive, lengthy operations like cataract removal, carried on without anesthesia, were a torture for both doctor and patient. Koller's discovery put an end to that. It immediately became common knowledge in the medical community, and there was sudden great interest in all aspects of cocaine. For example, the December 6, 1884, issue of the *British Medical Journal* had seven articles on cocaine; after a Dr. Squibb published a note about the drug in the *Philadelphia Medical Record,* he received 300 letters of inquiry from physicians. The use of cocaine anesthesia was quickly extended to other areas of surgery: rhinology, laryngology, gynecology, urology, dentistry. Before the end of the year 1884 H. Knapp was able to review a wide range of surgical uses.[21]

New forms of anesthesia that went beyond the topical application of cocaine solutions to body surfaces were almost immediately introduced. In 1884 William Halsted of Johns Hopkins invented nerve block, or conduction anesthesia, by injecting cocaine into nerve trunks. In 1885 J. Leonard Corning introduced regional anesthesia. Later Carl Ludwig Schleich produced infiltration anesthesia by subcutaneous injection (1892), and August Bier originated spinal anesthesia (1898). Although its potential toxicity was recognized early, until the end of the nineteenth century cocaine was the only available local anesthetic. It was not until 1899 that Einhorn synthesized procaine (Novocain), a substitute without cocaine's unpredictable and dangerous central nervous system effects.

Meanwhile, especially in the early years, cocaine was triumphing as what would now be disparagingly called a panacea. The same Corning who invented regional anesthesia declared, "Of all the tonic preparations ever introduced to the notice of the professions, this [coca] is undoubtedly the most potent for good in the treatment of exhaustive and irritative conditions of the central nervous system." [22] Considering the importance of the central nervous system in body functioning, this almost amounted to saying that coca is good for what ails you. Similar claims have been and are made for alcohol, opium, cannabis, LSD, and other drugs affecting the mind. But cocaine was the "drug of the eighties." Its promotion as a cure for morphine addiction and alcoholism was an example of a typical stage in the career of psychoactive drugs: their use to overcome the consequences of abuse of other psychoactive drugs. But cocaine was also used as a cure for many other ailments. From July to December of 1885, for example, there were 27 articles, notes, and letters on cocaine in the *New York Medical Journal*, recommending it for seasickness and trigeminal neuralgia, among other conditions. The drug house Parke Davis brought out its 101-page pamphlet, *Coca Erythroxylon and Its Derivatives*, in that year. Cocaine was adopted as the remedy of choice by the Hay Fever Association and recommended for head colds and "catarrh." William A. Hammond, a former Surgeon General of the United States Army, suggested coca wine for stomach irritability, "cerebral hyperemia due to excessive mental exertion," "the mental depression that accompanies hysteria in the female," and other morbid central nervous system conditions.[23] He thought pure cocaine even better than coca for most purposes, and recommended it for inflammations of the mucous membranes and to prevent masturbation in women by anesthetizing the clitoris.[24] Coca products were in use for such varied purposes for a generation or more.

The book *Peru: History of Coca*, published in 1901 by the American physician W. Golden Mortimer, sums up the favorable side of medical opinion about coca. Mortimer's recommendations for coca wine or coca extract and occasionally for cocaine are even more varied than Mantegazza's or Freud's. He approvingly mentions its use by French bicyclists and by a championship lacrosse team. (Apparently he saw no ethical problems in the use of drugs by athletes.) Contradicting Mantegazza's view that coca acts as a stimulant on the heart, he contends that it is primarily a regulator, calming an overexcited heart and strengthening a weak one. He believes that Mantegazza noticed only the central nervous system effect produced by cocaine and failed to observe the direct tonic effect of other coca alkaloids on the heart muscle. Mortimer was recommending coca for alcohol and opium addiction long after the use of cocaine in such cases was considered a disastrous mistake. A whole chapter on the history of music and voice production (the book tends to ramble) was apparently inspired by the popularity of coca preparations among singers. Mortimer also listed the results of a mail survey of prominent physicians; only a small minority of them used coca, but those who did considered it helpful for a large variety of illnesses.[25]

The use of a single drug for various and often vaguely defined conditions, as Mortimer's book and his correspondence show, was characteristic of that era. Cocaine's two distinct effects, as a local anesthetic and central nervous system stimulant, made it seem especially attractive. Mortimer devotes considerable space to a discussion of neurasthenia, a diagnosis that is no longer popular today. He describes its symptoms as headache of a special kind (a feeling of constriction over the back of the head), digestive troubles, incapacity for work, loss of sexual desire, muscular weakness and stiffness, back pain, insomnia, and "hypochondriacal views of life." Mortimer admits that this is a "combination of symptoms of very different nature" which requires a variety of different measures; he recommends coca as a useful adjunct in treatment.[26] Of course, doctors still commonly prescribe psychoactive drugs for very general functional disturbances: amphetamines and tranquilizers have been used in the same ways as coca (or opium, or alcohol). But it was even easier to use drugs this way at a time when pharmacological theories were more speculative and confused than they are now. It was a time of trial, groping, and uncertainty in medicine. Where drugs acting on the central nervous system are concerned, we may not have emerged from that stage of tentativeness as much as we sometimes think we have.

Mortimer dedicated his book to Angelo Mariani, the chemist and entrepreneur whose coca preparations were one of the most popular medicines of the era, calling him "a recognized exponent of the 'Divine Plant' and the first to render coca available to the world." Mariani was not only a promotional genius but a student of the history and folklore of coca; he cultivated coca plants in his own conservatories in Paris and distributed them to botanical gardens all over the world. He provided Mortimer with information and botanical specimens; Mortimer considered his coca preparations superior to all others in flavor and effectiveness. Mariani wrote several articles and monographs on coca which combine historical, botanical, and medical information with the promotion of his company's product. The most important of these was *Coca and Its Therapeutic Applications* (1890), which went through several editions. He sold coca extract not only as Vin Mariani but also as Elixir Mariani (stronger and with greater alcohol content than the wine), Pâte Mariani (a throat lozenge), Pastilles Mariani (Pâte Mariani with a little cocaine added), and Thé Mariani (concentrated coca leaf extract without wine).[27]

Mariani was not one of those manufacturers of proprietary medicines who advertised their products mainly to the general public. He was proud of the numerous and enthusiastic testimonials his coca preparations received from physicians, and his company approved of the moves made after the turn of the century toward restricting direct consumer advertising of drugs. He was able to cite prominent physicians like J. Leonard Corning, who declared his coca wine "the remedy par excellence against worry." He carefully pointed out that his drug was *"introduced solely through physicians"* (his italics) and could provide a list of about 3,000 physicians who recommended it. It won prizes and medals at various expositions, including one from England that called it "wine for athletes," and it received what Mariani says was an unsolicited recommendation from the Academy of Medicine of France. In the later years, when coca was beginning to lose its status as a respectable medicine, his company's American publication offered a reward for identification of defamers of Vin Mariani, declaring that a slur against it was a slur against the intelligence of many prominent physicians.[28]

Mariani's products were as popular with the public as with physicians. From the testimonials of eminent people he put together a "cyclopedia of contemporary biography" with a biographical sketch and portrait of each famous man or woman who testified to the virtues of Vin Mariani.[29] Thomas Edison (famous for his insomniac habits) was among them, and so was Pope Leo XIII, who presented Mariani with a gold medal and habitually carried a flask of the wine at his belt. The Czar of Russia, Jules Verne, Emile Zola, Henrik Ibsen, and the Prince of Wales also endorsed Mariani's wine. Mariani reports that doctors gave General Ulysses Grant, the former president of the United States, Thé Mariani, one teaspoon to a cup of milk per day, for five months during his last illness, in 1885. In their opinion, it prolonged his life and enabled him to complete his famous *Memoirs*.[30] Mariani's advertising made good use of the drug's popularity among actors and actresses, singers, and musicians. (No doubt he would have solicited athletes' testimonials more often if they had had the respectability and celebrity status they enjoy today.) Sarah Bernhardt, the composers Gounod and Massenet, and the *prima donna* Adelina Patti, among many others, praised Mariani's preparations. Entertainers never entirely stopped using cocaine, and its popularity in the worlds of theater, film, and popular music has probably never been greater than it is today. Little has been heard about coca extract itself in those or any other European and North American social groups since 1910, although a half-bottle of Vin Mariani, vintage 1880, was sold at a London wine auction in 1970 for four pounds.[31]

Cocaine was so popular with writers and intellectuals that an article entitled "The Influence of Cocaine on Contemporary Literary Style" appeared in the American journal *Current Literature* in 1910. It declared that cocaine was responsible for the "smooth and flowing sentences now so characteristic of the magazine writing of this period" and warned that cocaine addiction was increasing among the intellectual class.[32] This kind of (to put it mildly) speculative stylistic analysis constitutes most of the evidence we have of influence by cocaine on literary production. The drug is more likely to have simply given people the strength and will to write than to have provided content or style. We have mentioned Grant's *Memoirs*. Another literary work that may have been written with the help of cocaine is Robert Louis Stevenson's "The Strange Case of Dr. Jekyll and Mr. Hyde."

The facts are these. Stevenson wrote his famous story in three days and three nights, then burned the manuscript and rewrote it in another three days and nights. It was October 1885, and the British medical journals, eagerly read by Stevenson's wife, who hoped to find something to help her invalid husband, were full of articles on cocaine. Stevenson had been taking morphine, a drug not conducive to the production of 60,000 words in six days. His stepson later said, "The mere physical feat was tremendous; and instead of harming him, it roused and cheered him inexpressibly." Stevenson had fantasies and dreams about little creatures he called Brownies who gave him the inspiration for "Dr. Jekyll and Mr. Hyde." The story, of course, describes the transformation of an upright physician and scientist into a monster of immorality by a drug. None of Stevenson's letters or biographers mention cocaine. It is certainly conceivable that cocaine gave this sick man the energy that enabled him to write so much so fast. It is possible, though unlikely, that the Brownies were Lilliputian hallucinations of the kind sometimes induced by stimulant drugs like cocaine. And it might even be, although this is less likely still, that the plot of "Dr. Jekyll" owed something to the reports of cocaine abuse, especially among physicians, that were just beginning to appear.[33]

Mariani's coca preparations were the most famous among many on the market in the late nineteenth century. Parke Davis, for example, sold cocaine in cigarettes, in an alcoholic drink called Coca Cordial, and in sprays, ointments, tablets, and injections.[34] One of the most popular drinks containing coca extract was Coca-Cola, first concocted by John Styth Pemberton, a Georgia pharmacist, in 1886. Since cocaine is no longer an acceptable or legal stimulant, the Coca-Cola Company does not like to be reminded of this aspect of its early history. The author of a generally well-informed long article on Coca-Cola in *The New Yorker* implies that the presence of cocaine was accidental: "In its formative days, the drink did contain a minute quantity of cocaine, since this drug was not removed from the coca leaves that constituted a tiny fraction of its makeup." [35] This is totally misleading. Pemberton was a pharmacist and he sold Coca-Cola as a medicine: a headache remedy and stimulant that contained the "wonder drug" of those years, coca, as its main active principle. Pemberton had registered a trademark for a brew he called "French Wine of Coca, Ideal Tonic," possibly in imitation of Mariani, in 1885. In 1886 he removed the alcohol, added kola nut extract (which contains caffeine) and some citrus oils for flavor, renamed the product, and began to advertise it as "the intellectual beverage and temperance drink." In 1888 he replaced ordinary water with soda water, which was already associated with mineral springs and health.

Asa Griggs Candler, another pharmacist, bought all the rights to Coca-Cola in 1891 and founded the Coca-Cola Company in 1892. According to the author of a book on the history of pharmacy in Georgia, the soda fountain became an essential part of the retail drugstore in the United States mainly because of Coca-Cola, "the first generally advertised product that directed people to a drugstore." [36] Candler "believed in Coca-Cola with an almost mystical faith," according to his son, and he advertised it throughout the 1890s as a "sovereign remedy" as well as an enjoyable drink.[37] As late as 1903 a Colonel J. W. Watson of Georgia was quoted in the *New York Tribune* as urging legal action against "a soda fountain drink manufactured in Atlanta and known as Coca-Cola" because of its cocaine content.[38] But the men who ran the Coca-Cola Company were commercially astute enough to sense the change in public opinion that was to make cocaine a social outcast, and by the time the Pure Food and Drug Act was passed in 1906 they had taken it out of their drink and replaced it with caffeine. It is interesting to note that even in 1909 there were 69 imitations of Coca-Cola that contained cocaine.[39] People did not immediately forget the original basis of Coca-Cola's popularity: 40 or 50 years ago it was still possible to order a bottle by asking for a "shot in the arm."

The soda fountain in the drugstore where Coca-Cola was dispensed, a poor relative of the spa or watering place patronized by the upper classes in the nineteenth century, represents a kind of fusion of the health giving and the pleasure giving that is not necessarily unreasonable but may lead to disaster. That is what happened with cocaine almost as soon as doctors began to use it. We leave aside here the cases of acute poisoning and occasional death from its use as an anesthetic. They are important as part of the history of surgical anesthesia and for what they indicate about the physiological effects of cocaine, but they are not the reason it became an outlaw drug. Anesthesia was recognized to be a dangerous procedure in those days. General anesthetics like ether and chloroform killed more often than cocaine. All these drugs were used because there was no choice. When substitutes for cocaine became available, surgeons stopped using it except topically. Before that, they could only try to learn what precautions had to be taken about technique, dosage, and site of application. (Cocaine became a "drug menace" to the public not because it sometimes killed people in surgery but because what had been regarded as the very sign of its curative power, the pleasure it gave, became a source of what we now call drug dependence and drug abuse.)

Before 1885 there had been reports of acute cocaine intoxication, but physicians doubted the possibility of chronic abuse because many of the effects of large doses seemed frightening rather than alluring. (They were apparently not considering what alcoholics, for example, are willing to put up with for the sake of drink.) But they soon began to conclude that cocaine abuse was "a habit that develops more easily and destroys the body and soul faster than morphine." By 1890, at least 400 cases had been reported in the medical literature of acute and chronic physical and psychological disturbances caused by the drug.[40]

The earliest serious cases of abuse involved morphine addicts who took the cocaine cure recommended by Bentley and Freud. As early as May 1885 Ludwig Lewin, the famous student of psychotropic drugs and later the author of *Phantastica: Narcotic and Stimulant Drugs,* was expressing skepticism about this cure. He recognized that cocaine provided temporary symptomatic relief in morphine withdrawal but rejected Freud's view that it could serve as a substitute for the opiate. He also suspected that chronic use of cocaine in large doses could produce toxic effects. In the same year J. B. Mattison, in an article in the *New York Medical Journal* entitled "Cocaine in the Treatment of Opiate Addiction," agreed that its effect was transient and that there was genuine danger of producing a cocaine habit. By 1886 cases of cocaine psychosis with tactile hallucinations ("coke bugs") were appearing. In May of that year the *New York Medical Record* commented editorially: "No medical technique with such a short history has claimed so many victims as cocaine."[41]

Albrecht Erlenmeyer was probably the most important of the physicians who early observed the symptoms of acute and chronic cocaine intoxication and warned against the use of cocaine in morphine addiction. He issued his first warning in 1885 and returned to the subject in another article written in 1886 and an 1887 monograph on "Morphine Addiction and Its Treatment." Erlenmeyer melodramatically denounced cocaine as "the third scourge of mankind," after alcohol and morphine. He found that morphine addicts tended to add cocaine to morphine rather than replace the original drug, and he considered the combined morphine-cocaine habit worse than straight morphine. He described patients who "cured" themselves of morphine addiction with cocaine and then had to take morphine again to counteract the sleeplessness and mental confusion brought on by cocaine. Some of the symptoms he mentioned—insomnia, graphomania, paranoia (he states that three of his patients eventually had to be put in insane asylums)—were obviously, as we shall see, produced by cocaine if by any drug. Erlenmeyer pointed out that some observers had been confusing cocaine psychoses with morphine abstinence symptoms. He admitted that cocaine itself produced few abstinence symptoms except depression, but he concluded that of all drugs only alcohol could be as devastating.[42]

Erlenmeyer noted that all his cases involved a combination of morphine and cocaine abuse rather than cocaine alone, and most of the cocaine abusers in the next generation whose condition was serious enough to come to the attention of physicians or the law were also using opiates or alcohol. We will discuss the significance of this when we come to talk about the effects of cocaine in more detail. (What it does *not* mean is that cocaine is harmless unless combined with opiates, or that only opiate addicts and alcoholics are likely to abuse cocaine.) Historically, the fact that cocaine was not usually used alone helped to create a confusion between cocaine and opiates that made them both seem more fearful: the physical addictiveness of the opiates was ascribed to cocaine, and the psychological and physical effects of cocaine abuse were attributed to the opiates. The two quite different kinds of drug began to suffer similar legal restrictions and a similar decline in public and professional estimation.

At first physicians and the public made little distinction between cocaine and coca. Therefore the growing fear of cocaine changed attitudes toward coca, just as fear of morphine and heroin made opium smoking seem more dangerous. Advocates of coca then began to fight a rearguard action in its defense. They insisted (correctly) that coca never caused the kinds of disturbances that were ruining the reputation of the pure chemical cocaine, and (with less obvious justification) that it was not the cocaine in coca but the peculiar mixture of alkaloids that produced its characteristic effects. These themes are prominent in Mariani's and Mortimer's works. Mariani described his coca extract as consisting of "the soluble parts of the Peruvian plant" and stated that it could not produce what was then called cocainism because it did not contain the pure alkaloid cocaine. By 1906 the journal published in the United States by Mariani's company was insisting that Vin Mariani was "not a cocaine preparation" and was made from "sweet" leaves with only "an infinites-imal trace of the cocaine base." Mortimer extravagantly contended that cocaine no more fully represents the effect of coca than the prussic acid in peach pits represents the effect of peaches.[43] More reasonably, he claimed that some of coca's beneficial qualities, especially the cardiac, muscular, and digestive effects, should be attributed not to the action of cocaine on the central nervous system but to alkaloids affecting other organs directly. We will consider these matters—the evidence about them is sparse—when we discuss the effects of coca in more detail. In practice, the idea that coca is fundamentally different from cocaine never gained much influence in the medical community or among the public. And when coca extract went into decline as a medicine it did not become a recreational drug (although a sweet liqueur called Élixir de Coca is still sold in Peru). The kinds of people who had been drinking Mariani's wine took to sniffing cocaine in powder form; it seems that cocaine simply gave them more of whatever they thought they were getting from coca.

Physicians were the first to recognize the powers of cocaine and had the easiest access to it; they probably used and abused it, as they used and abused morphine, more than any other occupational group. In 1901, for example, it was estimated that 30 percent of the cocainists in the United States were doctors or dentists.[44] Probably the most famous case of cocaine abuse by a physician is that of the great surgeon William Halsted of Johns Hopkins (1852–1922), who invented nerve block anes-thesia. At the time of his first anesthesia experiments in 1884, according to his student Wilder Penfield, "cocaine hunger fastened its dreadful hold on him." There followed a "confused and unworthy period of medical practice," then a year's stay in a hospital and a curative sailing cruise. When he returned, "the brilliant and gay extravert seemed brilliant and gay no longer." [45] After a further hospital stay, he apparently recovered and stopped using cocaine. What no one knew at the time except Sir William Osler, who revealed it in a manuscript entitled "Inner History of Johns Hopkins Hospital" and first made public in 1969, long after his death, was that Halsted was taking three grains (200 mg) of morphine a day. He eventually reduced the dose to one and a half grains a day, but the "struggle against the dreadful discomfort of drug hunger" continued to the end of his life.[46]

There seems to be some confusion about exactly what Halsted's prob-lem was, since Osler also refers to a "cocaine and morphia habit." A recent article in the *Journal of the American Dental Association* trans-lates the three grains of morphine into three grains of cocaine. It looks as though the epidemic confusion between the two drugs is at work here.

Cocaine might have made Halsted a brilliant and gay extravert; the sedative morphine certainly did not. It appears that Halsted cured himself of the craving for cocaine, which was ruining his career, by means of morphine, which allowed him to function normally (as opiates often do), and paid the price of physical addiction.

Halsted remarks in a 1918 letter to Osler that three of his assistants became victims of the cocaine habit and died without recovering from it. In a later letter he states: "Yes, I published three or four little papers in 1884 and 1885 in the *New York Medical Journal* on the subject of cocaine anesthesia. They were not creditable papers for I was not in good form at the time." [47] One of these papers had the title "Practical Comments on the Use and Abuse of Cocaine, Suggested by Its Invariably Successful Employment in More than a Thousand Minor Surgical Operations." Its first sentence provides what might be one of the few genuine examples of "the influence of cocaine on contemporary literary style":

> Neither indifferent as to which of how many possibilities may best explain, nor yet at a loss to comprehend, why surgeons have, and that so many, quite without discredit, could have exhibited scarcely any interest in what, as a local anaesthetic, had been supposed, if not declared, by most so very sure to prove, especially to them, attractive, still I do not think that this circumstance, or some sense of obligation to rescue fragmentary reputation for surgeons rather than the belief that an opportunity existed for assisting others to an appreciable extent, induced me, several months ago, to write on the subject in hand the greater part of a somewhat comprehensive paper, which poor health disinclined me to complete.[48]

This syntax undoubtedly represents some kind of achievement. The reader can judge whether it is a successful employment of cocaine.

The greatest mind among the medical men who underwent the influence of cocaine belonged to Sigmund Freud. He first learned of it through Aschenbrandt's experiments on the Bavarian soldiers and the American reports of its use as a cure for morphine addiction. He refers to the drug in a letter to his fiancée, Martha Bernays, on April 21, 1884, as "a project and a hope" for reducing fatigue and counteracting morphine withdrawal symptoms. He started using it himself and called it a "magical drug," sending some to Martha "to make you strong and give your cheeks a red color." In May he began administering cocaine to his friend Ernst von Fleischl-Marxow as a substitute for the morphine he had been using to deaden phantom pain from an amputated thumb. At the time Freud wrote the paper "On Coca" (June 1884) he found the results encouraging. For several years he continued to use cocaine and experiment with it. He teased Martha about it: "You shall see who is stronger, a gentle little girl who doesn't eat enough or a great wild man who has cocaine in his body." He tested its effect on strength with a dynamome-ter—the only experimental study of his career—and found that it did not affect muscular capacity directly but produced a general sense of well-be-ing, improving performance most when he was tired or depressed. In general, small doses of cocaine had little effect on him when he was in generally good health but made him feel normal for four or five hours when he was below par. In a letter to Martha of February 1886, possibly written under the influence of cocaine, he referred to the relief it provided for his neurasthenia; he also told how it reduced his shyness in social sit-uations and even suggested that it made him feel as though he had the strength to sacrifice his life, like his ancestors defending the Temple. He was so well known as an authority that Parke Davis solicited his opinion on their cocaine; he pronounced it as good as the product of the German drug house Merck.[49]

As far as its effects on himself were concerned, Freud never had any reason to criticize cocaine. But his friend Fleischl took larger and larger amounts of the drug and began to suffer severe toxic symptoms. By the spring of 1885 he was taking one gram a day by subcutaneous injection and, in the words of Carl Koller, another friend, had become "a cocainist instead of a morphinist, probably the first of these unfortunates in Europe. And many a night have I spent with him watching him dig imag-inary insects out of his skin in his sensory hallucinations." Freud too spent "the most frightful night of his life" with Fleischl in a state of cocaine delirium in June of 1885. So when Erlenmeyer denounced co-caine as the "third scourge of mankind" and criticized Freud for encour-aging its use, feelings of sorrow and guilt as well as concern for his pro-fessional reputation were involved in the response.[50]

This last of Freud's cocaine papers, "Craving for and Fear of Cocaine," published in July 1887, is an interesting professional and personal docu-ment. It retreats from some of his former positions and defends others. He admits that cocaine should not be used in morphine addiction be-cause the habit that may ensue is "a far more dangerous enemy to health than morphine," producing quick physical and mental deterioration, paranoia, and hallucinations. But he insists that *all reports of addiction to cocaine and deterioration resulting from it refer to morphine addicts. . . . Cocaine has claimed no other, no victim on its own"* (Freud's ita-lics). (Of course, he did not know about Halsted.) He thought only mor-phine addicts were so weak in will power as to be susceptible to chronic cocaine abuse; he himself had felt no desire for continued use but on the contrary, "more often than I should have liked," an aversion to the drug.

He discussed acute poisoning and concluded that "the reason for the ir-regularity of the cocaine effect lies in the individual variations in excit-ability and in the variation of the conditon of the vasomotor nerves on which cocaine acts." He recommended abandoning subcutaneous injec-tion except as an anesthetic. Appended to the paper was a summary of a report to the New York Neurological Society by William Hammond, which recommended a cocaine-wine drink (not Mariani's coca wine) as a tonic and stimulant and for dyspepsia and injections of cocaine for "fe-male melancholia with mutism." [51] This paper was Freud's last profes-sional publication on cocaine, but in a letter to Ferenczi on June 1, 1916, he commented in connection with a prospective patient who used the drug that it could produce paranoid symptoms if taken to excess. He also remarked that drug abusers were bad risks in analysis because they found it too easy to cling to the security of their drug.[52]

Freud always regretted that he had not made the discovery of the use of cocaine in surgical anesthesia that brought fame to Koller. In *An Autobi-ographical Study* he attributes this failure, in what Ernest Jones regards as a disingenuous excuse, to the interruption of his work by a journey to visit his fiancée. In other contexts he admitted that he had simply been too lazy to pursue the matter. As Jones points out, Freud in any case thought of cocaine as a stimulant rather than an anesthetic and was more interested in its internal use than in any local application. Many years later Freud referred to his cocaine studies as a distracting hobby that took him far from his serious work in neuropathology. Jones attributes his in-tense interest and later guilt and need to inculpate his fiancée Martha to his having taken a surreptitious shortcut to dispel his depression and so "achieve virility and enjoy the bliss of union with the beloved." He had hoped to achieve fame and fortune by means of some application of the drug, so that he would be able to marry sooner. Instead, the fate of Fleischl gave him reason for self-reproach, and the discrediting of co-caine as a cure for morphine addiction and other ills damaged his reputa-tion and eventually made the acceptance of psychoanalysis even more difficult. Freud seldom referred to the cocaine episode later in his life.[53]

Nevertheless, Jürgen vom Scheidt, in an interesting recent article in a German psychoanalytic journal, [54] suggests that the psychophar-macological properties of cocaine may actually have aided Freud's self-analysis and contributed to the development of his ideas. The cocaine epi-sode was one of the most exciting times of Freud's life: the first patient who came to him on his own and not through the recommendation of a colleague had been attracted by the writings on cocaine; and the Ameri-can ophthalmologist Knapp, the author of a book on the surgical applications of the drug, had recognized and greeted him at the Salpêtrière in Paris as the author of "On Coca." It was during the time when he worked with Charcot in Paris, 1885 to 1886, that Freud began the transition from mainly physiological to mainly psychiatric interests. At that time he was using cocaine regularly and writing several papers about it. As a psycho-pharmacological agent, it may have mediated the change in Freud's in-terests. The letters to Martha from Paris show that cocaine also loosened Freud's censorship over the expression of his feelings, and even, in this period just before his marriage, relieved his neurasthenia, like the pres-ence of his fiancée; vom Scheidt notes that Freud more than once re-ferred to drugs as a substitute for sex. In his view the intoxicant impaired or changed Freud's ego-functions and released sexual and aggressive drives, producing a mild regression that made the inner world of dream and fantasy come forth more strongly; the unconscious wish for a deeper regression found an outlet in Freud's enthusiastic words about cocaine.

Vom Scheidt also provides new interpretations of the well-known fact that some of the most important dreams analyzed in *The Interpretation of Dreams* contain references to cocaine. Freud continued to prescribe cocaine until at least 1895, the year of his self-analysis, for topical appli-cation to the nasal mucous membranes, and he used it himself for sinusi-tis. He suffered not only from nasal infections but from migraine and, after an attack of influenza in 1889, heart arrhythmia (irregular heart ac-tion). Fliess induced him to give up smoking in 1894, and a short while afterward he suffered a severe cardiac condition with racing and irregular heart, tension, hot pain in the left arm, and respiratory difficulties. Fliess, who had previously diagnosed Freud's heart troubles as being of nasal or-igin, now attributed them to nicotine poisoning. Although Freud doubted the diagnosis, he managed to stop smoking for 14 months, until he could no longer tolerate abstinence. By this time Fliess had again decided that the heart condition was of nasal origin, and this conclusion was ap-parently supported by the improvement that followed an operation and the use of cocaine nose drops. Jones believes that the heart troubles, the migraine, and the nasal infections were all neurotic, although slightly aggravated by the effects of nicotine.[55] Vom Scheidt remarks that Freud spoke of his need for "something warm between the lips" and suggests that abstinence from tobacco aroused his oral drives and that he needed the kind of mild regression provided by cigars, and earlier by cocaine, to free his creativity.

The crucially important dream of "Irma's Injection" took place six weeks after Freud started smoking again. In his own analysis of this dream, Freud describes his use of cocaine for nasal congestion and mentions the case of a woman in whom it had caused necrosis of the nasal tissues. He also refers to the Fleischl affair and the reproaches he had incurred, stating that he had never intended Fleischl to inject the drug. Acccording to Freud, the thought of Fleischl showed defensive pride in his own conscientious handling of chemical substances. But vom Scheidt suggests that the unconscious conflict and guilt might have been related to Freud's own use of cocaine rather than Fleischl's. He notes that in his analysis Freud incorrectly states that he began to use the drug in 1885; actually, he began to *inject* it in 1885. Freud recalls, not here but in his analysis of the dream of the "Botanical Monograph" (itself a reference to his original paper on coca), that an eye operation was performed on his father for glaucoma in 1885 with the aid of cocaine. Vom Scheidt offers this interpretation of "Irma's Injection": if cocaine had affected his father the way it affected Fleischl, Freud would in effect have committed patricide; the injection of Irma is equivalent to impregnating Martha (she was pregnant at the time of the dream), which is equivalent to incest with his mother; so the use of cocaine is a symbolic expression of oedipal desires. Vom Scheidt finds cocaine references in seven other dreams analyzed by Freud, and remarks that this is not surprising, since cocaine was his most substantial intellectual project before psychoanalysis.

On this interpretation, cocaine euphoria helped to show Freud the way to his new conception of the mind. As primitive cultures use drugs to bring the believer into contact with divinity, Freud used cocaine to make contact with the realm of the unconscious. The drug was more than the distraction Freud later considered it to have been; it turned him off the common academic path and toward research of revolutionary originality. So vom Scheidt raises the possibility that cocaine left its greatest mark on the world by way of the mind of Freud. But even if that were so, it is doubtful how much should be attributed to the properties of the drug itself; alcohol, opium, or other drugs might have had the same effect in other historical circumstances. The psychopharmacological peculiarities of cocaine could not have been so important as the conjunction of intellect, personality, situation, and environment.[56]

The most famous, after Freud, of all the Victorian intellectuals who used cocaine was the fictional detective Sherlock Holmes. Sir Arthur Conan Doyle, his creator, was a physician who practiced for a while as an ophthalmologist. He must have been intimately acquainted with the properties of the drug and may have used it himself as a stimulant. Dr. Watson, Doyle's narrator, first mentions cocaine in *The Sign of the Four*, published in 1890. At that time Holmes was injecting a 7 percent solution intravenously three times a day—apparently a rather large dose. Since

Watson reports asking, when he saw Holmes with the needle, whether it was morphine or cocaine, Holmes seems to have had more than one drug habit. But we hear no more of morphine from Watson. In the spirit of mock scholarship with which Sherlock Holmes studies are conducted, we might guess that Holmes was one of those addicts who used cocaine to withdraw from morphine and simply replaced one drug with another. Holmes admitted that cocaine was bad for him physically but found it "transcendentally stimulating and clarifying to the mind." However, he did not use it when working on a case, but only to dispel boredom when he had nothing to do. In connection with a later case, "The Yellow Face," Watson again mentions the occasional use of cocaine as Holmes' only vice. After a while he began to see it as more than a casual indulgence. In "The Adventure of the Missing Three-Quarter," which ostensibly took place in about 1897, he refers to a "drug mania" that had threatened Holmes' career. Watson claims to have cured him of it, but says, "The fiend was not dead but sleeping." In later life, Holmes' only drug habit, like Freud's, was tobacco.[57]

Watson's fragmentary references to Holmes' cocaine habit, which most Holmes scholars regard as disappointingly inadequate considering that he was a medical man, have naturally excited considerable speculation. Some "authorities" contend that Professor Moriarty, the "Napoleon of crime" Holmes claimed to have destroyed, was a paranoid delusion brought on by the drug. In a recently published novel, *The Seven-Per-Cent Solution,* Nicholas Meyer builds an elaborate fiction on the idea that Watson sent Holmes to Freud in Vienna for a cure, which took place during the three years when Holmes had previously been supposed to be in hiding on the Continent after his alleged encounter with Moriarty and Moriarty's death. In spite of the considerable literature on Holmes, the experts have hardly begun to examine this obscure part of his fictional life.[58]

Cocaine's potentialities as a recreational drug soon became obvious; along with those older euphoriants and panaceas, opium and alcohol, it now became a drug with a dubious social reputation. In the 1890s, although people continued to inject cocaine and take it in drinks, sniffing or snorting it in powder form was discovered to be a particularly easy and efficient method of administration. Its use spread downward as well as upward in the class structure, in both Europe and the United States, and became especially common in the regions where the fringes of high society overlap with the fringes of bohemia and the lower middle class. Its users were described as "bohemians, gamblers, high- and low-class prostitutes, night porters, bellboys, burglars, racketeers, pimps, and casual laborers." In the United States bartenders put it into whiskey on request and peddlers sold it door to door. There were circles in which everyone carried cocaine and treated it as a luxury like cognac.[59]

There are several glimpses of patterns of cocaine use in the medical and lay press of the early twentieth century. An article on "The Increase of the Use of Cocaine among the Laity in Pittsburgh" in the *Philadelphia Medical Journal* for 1903 mentioned a druggist who sold it to railroad engineers for overtime work. This article also asserted that black convicts favored the drug. Negroes in Pittsburgh called one thoroughfare "Cocaine Street." Catarrh cures sold with glass tubes for sniffing were one source of the habit. Cocaine was supposed to be sold only on prescription but in fact was rather freely dispensed. W. B. Meister, in "Cocainism in the Army," published in *Military Surgeon* in 1914, mentions such means of obtaining cocaine as buying it from a prostitute who got it from a wholesale drug company by posing as a local druggist, and diverting it via the *ad libitum* refillable prescription of a laundry-truck driver. Meister suggested that a soldier who seemed too talkative or "egotistical and morose" might be using the drug.[60]

Various articles in the American press also give some idea of the kind of censorious attitude that was becoming more common. A 1908 article in the *New York Times,* "The Growing Menace of Cocaine," declared that cocaine "wrecks its victim more swiftly and surely than opium." It was easily available in patent medicines and popular among Negroes in the South, where "Jew peddlers" sold it to them. The lower classes were said to indulge in "sniff parties." A Father Curry was quoted as saying that because of cocaine and opium, drugstores were a greater menace than saloons. J. Leonard Corning, the anesthetics pioneer, now called cocaine "one of the most useful and at the same time one of the most dangerous agents" in the pharmacopoeia and warned against its use as a stimulant, especially by "neurotic persons," who were especially susceptible to the habit. Another physician asserted that no one was more degraded than the cocaine habitué: nothing could be done for the "coke fiend" and he was best left to die. In an article printed in 1911 the *Times* stated that cocaine was used to corrupt young girls and caused criminal acts and resistance to arrest. By 1914 the Atlanta police chief was blaming 70 percent of the crimes on cocaine, and the District of Columbia police chief considered it the greatest drug menace. When a drug has become so convenient as an explanation for crime, society is ready for prohibition.[61]

Pharmacists concerned for their reputations began to worry about cocaine early. In September 1901, at a meeting of the American Pharmacological Association, Vice-President S. F. Payne brought up the issue

of "Negro cocainists." The association set up a Committee on the Ac-
quirement of the Drug Habit, which reported to it in 1902 and again in
1903. The 1903 report combines straightforward racial prejudice with
the kind of reasonable concern about the overprescription of psychoactive
drugs that some physicians have been expressing recently in connection
with amphetamines, barbiturates, and tranquilizers. Here are some quotations: "Georgia reports almost every colored prostitute is addicted to
cocaine"; "Maryland reports sale of cocaine by disreputable physicians";
"Indiana reports that a good many negroes and a few white women are
addicted to cocaine"; "The negroes, the lower and criminal classes, are
naturally most readily influenced." Nothing, the report says, is more
baneful than cocaine. It turns upright men into thieves and liars. Drugstores fill prescriptions for it too freely and manufacturers supply it to retail stores even when they know it is being diverted to recreational use.
The report blames patent-medicine manufacturers but also a society that
wants quick solutions to its problems and thinks any medicine that is
taken at a soda fountain and makes one "feel so bright" must be harmless.[62] All this, racial prejudice aside, will sound familiar to anyone who
knows the career of amphetamines in 1940–1970: the more things
change, the more they remain the same, although amphetamines may
never attain the status of an outlawed drug menace.

It is obvious by now that the race issue, exposed sometimes directly
and sometimes in the guise of a fear of crime, appears prominently in the
condemnations of cocaine. Just as opium was associated with the Chi-
nese in the drive to outlaw it, so cocaine was associated with blacks. For a
while employers made it available to black workers, as the Spanish in
Peru had given the Indians coca. According to an article in the *British
Medical Journal,* for example, stevedores and cotton pickers in Louisiana
were supplied with cocaine. But soon whites came to see the drug as
more dangerous than useful. They thought it increased the cunning and
strength of blacks and enhanced their tendency toward violence—
especially, of course, sexual violence against white women. Colonel J. W.
Watson of Georgia, the man who had issued the stern warning about
Coca-Cola, now said that cocaine sniffing "threatens to depopulate the
Southern States of their colored population." [63] Anyone concerned with
the more sensational and ludicrous aspects of the racial situation at that
time may be interested in knowing that some whites believed cocaine
made blacks invulnerable to bullets—a concern that seems to be the opposite of Colonel Watson's. In any case, the cocaine-crazed black dope
fiend played an important role in the campaign to prohibit the drug.

Naturally, then, many people think that racial prejudice inspired the hostility toward cocaine. This idea has been revived in recent court cases involving the drug, because claims of racial discrimination have become one of the most effective ways of challenging established legal classifications. But we suspect that racial prejudice was ancillary. When respectable people decided that cocaine was a dangerous drug, they were inclined to concentrate on what used to be called the dangerous classes—the poor, especially blacks. After all, the same moves toward prohibiting the use of cocaine were made in Europe, where there was no racial issue. In fact, blacks probably used cocaine, like other prescription drugs, less than whites, simply because they had less money and less access to physicians. A report in 1914 on 2,100 consecutive black admissions to a Georgia insane asylum, for example, indicated that only two were cocaine users, and even for them cocaine had nothing to do with the reasons for admission.[64] Of course, the actual incidence of cocaine use among blacks must have been higher than that; but the special association of cocaine with blacks, unlike the association of opium with Orientals, was probably baseless. (Later it became more plausible.) Prohibitionists argued that keeping whiskey out of the hands of blacks would be beneficial for the white population, but that hardly meant the movement to abolish the use of alcohol was *inspired* by racism. The case of cocaine was similar. With cocaine, as with alcohol and opium, the dangerous classes also included white women, who were said to be subject to temptation, seduction, and corruption. In actual fact, the best-documented (if not the most severe) cases of cocaine abuse were white professional men, especially physicians.

It was some time before the patchwork of laws instituted to restrict the sale of cocaine actually reduced its availability much. In the United States, where cocaine sniffing was apparently more common than anywhere else, Oregon passed the first restrictive law in 1887. Before World War I most states made cocaine a prescription medicine and required that records of the prescriptions be retained for inspection. By 1912, 14 states had ordered "drug education" in the schools to warn about cocaine and opiates. Cocaine was actually considered more dangerous than opiates. The Proprietary Association of America, bidding for respectability and trying to fight disclosure laws, refused to permit the company that manufactured Dr. Tucker's Asthma Specific, a cocaine nostrum, to join. By 1914, 46 states had laws controlling the sale of cocaine and only 29 had laws controlling the sale of opiates; often the penalties for cocaine were harsher. In 1907 New York, under the leadership of Assemblyman Al Smith, passed a harsh cocaine law that made it almost impossible for physicians or patent medicine manufacturers to dispense the drug legally.] This law expressed the attitude of total condemnation that was about to become dominant.[65]

The federal government made its first move with the Pure Food and Drug Act of 1906, which forbade interstate shipment of food and soda water containing cocaine or opium and required that medicines containing these drugs be properly labeled. It also put the first restrictions on imports of coca leaves. But the sanctions were not severe, and the loophole for patent medicines was large. [In 1914 Congress passed the Harrison Narcotic Act, and it became the cornerstone of federal policy on cocaine for 50 years. It stipulated that anyone producing or distributing opiates or cocaine must register with the federal government and keep records of all transactions. Anyone handling the drugs was required to pay a special tax; thus the law could be enforced by a federal agency, the Bureau of Internal Revenue. Possession of opiates or cocaine by an unregistered person was not in itself a crime but was evidence of violation of the regulatory and tax provisions of the law. Unregistered persons could buy the drugs only on prescription from a physician for legitimate medical use. (This provision became important in connection with the opiates when later Supreme Court decisions declared "maintaining" an addict to forestall withdrawal symptoms not a legitimate medical purpose, but it never made much difference to official policy on cocaine.) The Harrison Act at first exempted some opiate preparations but none that contained cocaine. European countries, partly under prodding by the United States government, eventually imposed similar sanctions.]

Ever since then, our legal machinery has been pressing down on cocaine and the opiates alike. If anything, cocaine has been more heavily penalized. It was included with opiates in the order that set up the maintenance clinics that operated in 1919–1923, but in practice the clinics rarely dispensed cocaine because people who used only cocaine did not feel the physical need that drove opiate addicts to them. In New York, for example, the clinic stopped dispensing it after the first day. An exception was Albany, where 113 of 120 addicts in May 1920 were being given two grains (130 mg) of cocaine a day as well as an average of seven and a half grains of morphine.[66] In 1922 Congress prohibited most importation of cocaine and coca leaves and officially defined cocaine as a narcotic for the first time.* By 1931 every state had placed severe restrictions on the sale

* Federal law still classifies cocaine as a narcotic. Etymologically, this seems wrong, since the term is derived from the Greek word for "benumb" or "stupefy" and implies sedation or analgesia rather than stimulation. But for a long time it has been applied loosely to a great variety of drugs, possibly because numbing is thought of as something like "enabling one to forget one's troubles" and possibly because the most venerable psychoactive drugs—alcohol, opium, and cannabis—in fact often have a sedative effect.

of cocaine and 36 states made unauthorized possession a crime. The Uniform Narcotic Drug Act, proposed in 1932, was eventually adopted by all states except California and Pennsylvania and dominated official policy on cocaine, along with the Harrison Act, until 1970. Besides the usual criminal penalties for possession it required licensing for the manufacture and distribution of cocaine and detailed records of sales and prescriptions.

The federal government, meanwhile, continued to pursue the policy of suppression it had instituted with the Harrison Act. There were no substantial changes in this law from 1922 to 1951; then an amendment made prison sentences for possession mandatory and imposed the same penalty for failure to register as for importation of large amounts. In 1956 penalties were increased again. The Narcotics Manufacturing Act of 1960 required manufacturers of cocaine to register with the secretary of the treasury, who was empowered to license them and to set quotas on production. Finally, in 1970 the old federal drug laws were replaced by the Comprehensive Drug Abuse Prevention and Control Act, which in effect reenacted the existing control schedules under a new terminology. Coca and cocaine are classified, along with a number of opiates, barbiturates, and amphetamines, as Schedule II: high abuse potential with restricted medical use. Since cocaine is treated as a narcotic, the penalties are the same as those for morphine and other medical opiates and higher than those for non-opiates in the same Schedule: for illegal manufacture, distribution, or possession with intent to sell, up to 15 years in prison and a fine of $25,000; for possession with intent to use, up to one year and

---

The title of von Bibra's book, *Die Narkotischen Genussmittel und der Mensch*, published in 1855, may be translated as *The Narcotic Drugs and Man*, although "Genussmittel" literally means "means of enjoyment" or "luxury." Among the drugs it discusses are the stimulants tobacco, coffee, tea, coca, and mescaline. We have already mentioned the reference of a British medical journal in the 1870s to coca as "a new narcotic and a new stimulant." Freud, more etymologically scrupulous, contrasts stimulants like cocaine with narcotics, but he classes cannabis with opium as a narcotic. We would not do this today, although it is far more plausible than using the term for cocaine, which numbs only the tongue and palate. It would still be more plausible to call alcohol, barbiturates, and tranquilizers narcotics, although, unlike opiates, they are less effective against pain than against anxiety. No one does so, of course, since the term *narcotic* no longer has the vague but morally neutral connotations it had in the nineteenth century. It is used in public discourse today mainly to denounce a drug as a menace to society that must be suppressed. (Something similar has happened to the word *addiction*, which originally meant simply a habitual inclination.)

Jerome H. Jaffe, in his chapter on "Narcotic Analgesics" in Louis Goodman and Alfred Gilman's *The Pharmacological Basis of Therapeutics*, 4th ed. (New York: Macmillan, 1970), explicitly defines the term as interchangeable with "opioids" (p. 237). This clarifies matters, but it might be still better to drop the term "narcotic" entirely and simply speak of opiates, barbiturates, alcohol, or whatever depressant drug one has in mind. In any case, applying it to cocaine only promotes the confusion between cocaine and the opiates and an irrational, excessive social prejudice against both drugs. Another prejudicial term to be avoided, incidentally, is "hard drug," which has no meaning in medicine. This phrase sometimes seems to mean "anything illegal except cannabis" and takes no account of the very "hard" time many people have with legal drugs.

$1,000. There is no mandatory minimum sentence for possession. A Uniform Controlled Substances Act, designed to complement the Comprehensive Drug Abuse Prevention and Control Act, has been adopted by many states, with some variations in penalties; for example, simple possession of cocaine is only a misdemeanor in Idaho, but in Missouri sale to a minor may carry the death penalty. In 1973 New York State passed one of the harshest laws, making a life sentence mandatory for possession of more than two ounces of cocaine, with parole provisions reducing potential time served to not less than 15 years.[67]

International developments have been parallel. A series of International Conferences on Opium took place, largely at the urging of the United States government, at Shanghai and The Hague in the years before passage of the Harrison Act. In 1914, 44 nations attending the Third Hague Conference signed The Hague Opium Convention providing for strict restraints on the production, manufacture, and distribution of opiates and cocaine. The United States and a few other countries ratified this convention in 1915, and the rest of the world ratified it in 1919, when it became part of the Versailles Treaty. Since then the international legal machinery has been in principle as dedicated to the suppression of cocaine as the United States government. A series of treaties culminating in the United Nations Single Convention on Narcotic Drugs of 1961 has amplified and elaborated the control system. The Single Convention regulates the opium poppy, the coca bush, the cannabis plant, and their derivatives, replacing all predecessor treaties. It authorizes use of these drugs only for medical and scientific purposes and permits their cultivation, manufacture, possession, sale, distribution, import, and export only by government agencies or under government licenses, with strict supervision and record-keeping requirements. Although the Peruvian and Bolivian governments have approved this treaty and created formal monopolies to regulate the coca trade, it has been nearly impossible to enforce the restrictions. A 1972 amendment, not yet in effect, strengthens the International Narcotics Control Board and increases its authority to insure compliance with the treaty by national governments.

Between 1930 and the late 1960s the use of cocaine and medical and general interest in the drug seem to have declined greatly. Gerald T. McLaughlin writes, "Before 1930, cocaine, rather than heroin or opium, was viewed as the primary drug menace in the United States." A French author estimates that in 1924 there were 80,000 victims of *cocaïnomanie*—a term that suggests chronic cocaine intoxication but may mean any use of cocaine at all—in Paris alone, and only 20,000 drug abusers (*drogués*) of all kinds in all of France in 1971. (Obviously he excludes alcohol.) A 1926 article in the *New York Times* entitled "Cocaine Used Most by Drug Addicts" announced that 60 percent of the criminals in a Welfare Island workhouse were "drug addicts," most of them taking cocaine.[68] Most of the books that deal with cocaine as a social issue or a clinical problem were published in the 1920s; most of the novels, stories, and memoirs that show familiarity with its recreational use are from the same period. Even in the first decade of the new drug culture's flowering, cocaine remained relatively unpopular—expensive, rarely available, bracketed with heroin as a drug to be avoided. But around 1970 a revival of interest and respect began, comparable to the events of those decades at the end of the last century when cocaine was first introduced to the West.

3

COCAINE IN
AMERICA TODAY

Preliminaries

Before discussing the present and future position of cocaine in our society, we must offer some apologies. It is a subject very difficult to write about without guesswork, distortion, and false emphasis. Use of cocaine, like use of most other drugs, covers a good deal of social territory; what could be stated accurately for one corner of it would be misleading about the rest. Because cocaine is illegal, everything about its social status remains half-concealed; because the large-scale interest in it is so recent, there has been little time for a new descriptive literature to accumulate. It is impossible to find out the true extent of the illicit traffic; no substantial public surveys on cocaine use and users are available; even arrest statistics are unreliable, because the Federal Bureau of Investigation continues to lump cocaine with opiates (as a "narcotic") in its Uniform Crime Reports. Most important of all, the situation is changing fast; no stable pattern has yet emerged either in the use of the drug or in attitudes toward it. What we write today may seem naive or outdated in a year or two. In this kind of situation two poses are common: the spurious knowingness of the insider who imagines his own experience to be more extensive or more representative than it is; and the journalistic sensationalism of the outsider cashing in on the shock value of illicit drug use.

These attitudes reinforce each other, and we would like to avoid both. We describe the transient and obscure surface features of the present social situation not so much for their own sake as to place our later description of the effects of cocaine in a cultural context.

One topic usually considered to be an integral part of the sociology of contemporary drug use is clearly of more permanent interest than the latest fashion or scandal. This is the problem defined as "the motivation of the user." Unfortunately, in studies of illicit drug use the answer to an apparently sensible question is often pursued in a confusing and misleading way. In this case, it can degenerate into attempts to find ways to impute psychological abnormalities or moral deficiencies to those who use a socially disapproved drug. Consider two relatively harmless substances, marihuana and coffee. Only corporate marketing research divisions have shown much interest in why people drink coffee; but sociologists, psychiatrists, and—more ominously—police agencies are interested in the motivation of the user of marihuana. It is false to imply that something must be wrong with anyone who wants to ingest a chemical that has been declared legally out of bounds.

The question of why people want to use a drug, formulated in a general way, is both too simple and too complex to be very useful. The simple answer is to describe the effects and point out that they are desirable. So the mildly derisive "explanation" some marihuana smokers give to sociologists who want to study their motivations is that the stuff makes them feel good, or some elaboration of that idea. On the other hand, what the researcher means when he speaks of motivation may have nothing to do with what people think or say they want. He may be concerned with a causal chain based on some idiosyncratic concatenation of individual psychology, cultural norms (including the way in which the use of the drug is defined in a particular society—its folklore and mystique), and the availability of the drug. In that case the answer to the question of motivation becomes part of the biography of the user and the history of the culture. In this sense, as opposed to the derisively simple sense we mentioned before, there is no single motivation or easily classifiable set of motivations for sniffing cocaine or smoking marihuana any more than for drinking alcohol or coffee.

In other words, motivation tends to be either obvious or irrelevant, and the term is too often used for the dubious purpose of setting apart a peculiar class of drug users from respectable society as outcasts and scapegoats. The search for motivation is properly redirected or transformed into three other projects: description of the drug's psychological and physiological effects; analysis of the difficult problem of so-called dependence, habituation, and addiction; and observation of the conditions and circumstances in which the drug is available at a given time in a given society. We began this last project in the first two chapters and continue it in this one.

Background to the Contemporary Scene

Between 1930 and the late 1960s, recreational use of cocaine (except in South America) was largely out of sight and out of mind. There are several plausible reasons for the decline of interest. New restrictions on importation, manufacture, and distribution were introduced; substitutes were found for many of the surgical and prescription uses of cocaine; amphetamines appeared on the market in 1932 and provided a stimulant that was cheaper, more accessible, and longer-lasting, if less attractive to connoisseurs; the Depression made luxuries like cocaine less available. Whether as a cause or a consequence of the decline of interest, the sources of supply seem to have dried up. From about 1910 to 1930, a large proportion of the coca used to manufacture cocaine for medicinal purposes was cultivated in Java. The amount grown there reached a high of 1,676,000 kg in 1920 and began to fall, slowly through the 1920s and then precipitously; by 1938 Java was producing only 41,000 kg of coca, and after World War II cultivation was not resumed.[1] (Coca production in Peru fell from 1930 to 1935, but then began to rise again, until by 1938 it had surpassed the 1929 high of 5,500,000 kg; it has continued to rise until the present.)[2] It appears that until 1930 most of the cocaine in recreational use was diverted or supplied illegally and quasi-legally from pharmaceutical houses, drugstores, hospitals, and doctors' offices. When it was no longer manufactured in large quantities as a medicine, lovers of the drug had nowhere to go until the demand became great enough to generate a new refining and marketing network entirely outside of medical channels.

The background of this demand and the social situation it has created is a combination of old elites and the new drug culture. As a prescription drug, cocaine was most used by those who had access to the source and could pay the fees—physicians, lawyers, writers, preachers, actors, musicians, and other professional people, as well as the idle rich. When it was removed from soda drinks and patent medicines and legally restricted in other ways, the price rose and its use became even more confined to the rich or well connected. To the extent that it was available at all, cocaine became a plaything of the more adventurous and less respectable among the wealthy. Marcel Proust in *A la recherche du temps perdu* refers to its use in Parisian high society before 1914 and in a homosexual brothel during World War I. (He may have used it himself to relieve his asthma.) The drug was a familiar part of Cole Porter's café-society world of the 1930s, when he is said to have written a version of "I Get a Kick Out of You," his famous song of put-on weary decadence (for a musical comedy set in the 1920s), in which he included the line "Some get their kicks from cocaine." In Hollywood and around Broadway cocaine remained available if not abundant. Richard Ashley estimates, on the basis of correspondence with old-timers, that it was used in these circles in the 1920s about as much as marihuana among the middle class in general in 1970—it was not so familiar as to be taken for granted.[3] Cocaine plays a role, usually humorous, in a few early Hollywood films. In a 1916 parody of the Sherlock Holmes stories, starring Douglas Fairbanks, a manic detective named Coke Ennyday who is continually sniffing an unnamed white powder foils a ring of opium smugglers. Charlie Chaplin's *Modern Times* (1936) includes a scene in a jail cell where the tramp sniffs something identified as "nose powder" and becomes a comic superman. A low-budget 1939 film called *The Cocaine Fiends,* ostensibly a dire warning against the drug menace in the melodramatic vein of the better-known *Reefer Madness,* is now believed by some cognoscenti to have been a deliberate parody or joke; it has been revived recently for the sophisticated pleasure of the new cocaine users.

When cocaine went underground its status changed among the poor as well as the rich. It was even less available to the solid working-class citizen than to the solid middle-class citizen; but a few socially marginal members of the lower class, like the socially marginal upper-class groups we have just discussed, found ways of obtaining it. This is always the way with illicit drugs, and it is often misinterpreted as evidence that they are a cause of crime. In fact, even when cocaine was relatively freely available as a prescription drug, the poor could not use it very much if they were strictly law-abiding. When it became almost impossible to obtain legally, its associations became criminal; those who had least general respect for the law and conventional society were most likely to be persuaded of its virtues and to know where it could be found. Evidence that criminals use more of cocaine and other illicit drugs than the rest of the population must always be considered in this light.

The worlds of the unconventional rich and the unconventional poor who used cocaine were of course connected—not only by the quasi-conspiratorial nature of the drug traffic, but also by more general social associations. (Gamblers, prostitutes, actors, musicians, journalists, and artists might belong to either world and pass freely between them) In the United States, blacks in particular may have been an important part of this nexus. They were in a permanent condition of social marginality by virtue of skin color and for obvious reasons had little respect for white-imposed laws. If recent surveys are accurate, blacks still use cocaine proportionately more often than whites (although the cocaine they use may be weaker); the situation has probably been that way since 1930 and possibly since the Harrison Act, although evidence is even scarcer here than in other areas of the history of cocaine. In any case, black jazz musicians and other entertainers began to exert cultural influence in the world of white popular music and show business in general during the 1920s; the interest extended to the drugs they used, whether marihuana, heroin, or cocaine. During the period from 1930 to the late 1960s, all these cultural associations of cocaine—with the rich, with show business, with blacks— remained in memory and helped to shape the new cocaine market created by an unprecedented set of social circumstances.

These circumstances involved a profound alteration in the public attitude toward illicit drugs, at least among a large and influential minority. To describe fully how this came about would be impossible without analyzing the general upheaval that began in American society in the early 1960s. We can only gesture toward the subject by referring to the loss of respect for established institutions and moral attitudes among important parts of the middle class, the bohemianization of middle-class youth (the hippie rebellion and its camp followers), the introduction of psychedelics and the spread of marihuana use, with attendant drug ideologies and religions, the growing respect for black culture, and in general the process by which the attitudes and practices of avant-garde and fringe groups were taken over by a large section of the public and became familiar to an even larger section. It was inevitable that in the search for new pleasure drugs that ensued, cocaine would be rediscovered and rise to high social visibility. In a sense, all the old social scenes where cocaine had been used were merged on an enlarged public stage. Only a few other developments were necessary before it became fashionable again. Disillusionment with amphetamines, combined with legal restrictions that made them less freely available, was probably important; and a smuggling and marketing network had to be created with the help of Cuban exiles and other Latin Americans who had connections in Peru and Bolivia.

The Cocaine Traffic Today

Although coca was once cultivated in many parts of the tropics, today all the legal and illegal cocaine that reaches North America and Europe comes from its homeland in South America. Illegal cocaine is also refined almost exclusively in Latin America. The only firm licensed to import coca leaves into the United States is a chemical corporation that removes the alkaloids and sells them to pharmaceutical houses, then passes on the residue to the Coca-Cola Company for use as a flavoring agent. In response to our written request for information, this firm, the Stepan Chemical Company of Maywood, New Jersey, stated in a letter: "It is the policy of our firm not to reveal any information concerning our procurement, manufacturing, and selling operations for any of the products that we produce." According to the International Narcotics Control Board, world legal manufacture of cocaine amounted to 889 kg in 1973, all of it in the United States; legal consumption (as a local anesthetic) in the United States was 279 kg.[5] This is only a small fraction of the amount consumed illegally, and could not possibly be a significant source of illicit traffic.

The cocaine used for recreation in North America and Europe is grown in Peru, Bolivia, and Columbia and refined in clandestine laboratories in those countries and in Chile, Ecuador, and Argentina. (This may be changing. An illicit processing laboratory in California was seized by the federal government's Drug Enforcement Agency in 1975.)[6] A 1975 article in the *New York Times* tells of an Aymara Indian in a coca-growing region of Bolivia who owns a plot that produces 300 pounds of leaves a year, worth about $250. This will yield about 1 kg of cocaine, sold for $75,000 at retail prices in New York. First coca paste or crude cocaine is extracted; this may be transported to Chile or Colombia for further refining and conversion to cocaine hydrochloride. The cocaine hydrochloride crystal or powder is then smuggled by way of Central America to California or directly into San Antonio, Miami, or New York, where it is sold especially in Latin bars and restaurants. Large-scale smugglers often use bulk freight like coffee. Smaller independent operators may use private boats and planes or employ individual carriers called "mules" or "camels" who use such ingenious methods as soaking their clothes in a cocaine solution or swallowing condoms that contain the powder. (Occasional stories appear in the newspapers about smugglers who die when the condoms burst in their stomachs.) In the United States cocaine may be sold to middlemen who supervise cutting (dilution) and packaging in secret "coke mills" (where workers can earn as much as $300 a day) and then distribute the drug for retail sale. At retail, it is often sold by the "spoon," a variable amount of powder averaging about one-quarter of a measuring teaspoon, or half a gram; the cocaine content, of course, may be much lower.[7]

The dimensions of this trade are naturally obscure, but it is clear that the quantity of illicit cocaine on the market has been increasing rapidly since about 1970. In 1970 the federal government seized 305 pounds; in 1971 it seized 787 pounds. Seizures by the Berkeley, California, police department went up one-third in the same period. In New York City there were 874 arrests for sale or possession of cocaine in 1970 and 1,100 arrests in 1971; the amount seized by police had already gone up five times from 1969 to 1970.[8] Bureau of Customs seizures rose from 11 pounds in 1960 to 199 pounds in 1969 and 619 pounds in 1972. The amount of cocaine taken by federal agents first exceeded the amount of heroin in 1970, and in 1974 a Bronx prosecuting attorney declared that it had supplanted heroin as the main "drug of abuse" in New York City. The increase in total police seizures from 1969 to 1974 was sevenfold, and the Drug Enforcement Administration is now devoting half its efforts to cocaine.[9] It goes without saying that police seizures are only a tiny fraction of the amount actually on the market.

Prices in the illicit drug trade are subject to wild disparities and irregularities, but there is no doubt about the great financial cost of using cocaine and the enormous profits to be made from dealing in it. A man we interviewed who was familiar with the local market in the United States spoke of "people who like being involved with big cash" and "the hook of making that easy money," which he regarded as more dangerous than the hook of the drug itself. In late 1973 *Newsweek* quoted a Drug Enforcement Administration official as saying, "In the last three years, the coke traffic has gone right through the roof. Right now, *anybody* can go down there, turn a kilo for $4,000, and sell it back here for $20,000." One Mexican citizen arrested in the United States in 1972 for selling cocaine posted a cash bond of $250,000 and then disappeared.[10] This kind of money entices a growing number of people into the business. An article in the *Journal of Psychedelic Drugs* describes the advantages of cocaine dealing from the point of view of a former heroin addict and heroin dealer who had stopped using and selling opiates with the help of a methadone maintenance program. At the time of the interview he was using three spoons (a gram or two) of cocaine a day and claimed a net income of $3,000 to $4,000 a week:

I deal coke because you associate with a better class of people. I sell to executives, teachers, businessmen, pimps. I don't have to fuck around with low-life junkies, always sniffin' and scratchin' and always a dollar short beggin' to get a ping off your cotton. Shit, who ever heard of a swag [heroin] dealer workin' the X [a luxury apartment house]. Some of my best customers live in there. . . . I've got what I always wanted, I got my Mark IV, I've got my pick of any bitch on the strip and I've got a piece of a legitimate business in "A" [a resort city]. I'm OK now.[11]

Figures from various sources will give some idea of the current prices and profits. The cocaine dealer "Jimmy," portrayed in Richard Woodley's study *Dealer: Portrait of a Cocaine Merchant,* bought 425 grams of pure cocaine in New York for $4,400 in 1970. By 1972, according to a *New York Times* article, a "key" (kilogram) of cocaine worth $1,000 in Arica, Chile, might sell for $23,000 in New York. In reporting the capture of a ring of smugglers in late 1974, the *New York Times* gave the estimated wholesale price in New York as $10,000 a pound, or $24,000 a kilogram. Couriers were said to get $1,500 a kilogram. Recently a New York policeman was indicted for pocketing $15,000 in "buy money" that was supposed to be exchanged for 500 grams of cocaine.[12]

Retail prices are even more outrageously inflated. The heavily cut cocaine sold by "Jimmy" in 1970 was priced at $150 a tablespoon (not to be confused with a "spoon"). A "two-and-two" (two "lines" or snorts for each nostril) was worth $10, and it would cost "Jimmy" about $50 to "coke up" for an evening's pleasure. In 1972 cut cocaine was said to be selling for $500 to $1,500 an ounce, or $50 a gram. The PharmChem Research Foundation reported that the street price of samples assayed in late 1975 averaged in the range of $1,000 to $1,800 an ounce, or $45 to $85 a gram. The prices were not necessarily correlated with the degree of purity, which varied greatly. If price is measured by the cost in dollars per minute spent under the drug's influence, cocaine is probably ten times as expensive as heroin. It is cheaper in South American cities, and North Americans sometimes go there simply to get it. Several of the people we interviewed had made a trip to Colombia mainly for this purpose; one woman bought an ounce of pure cocaine there in 1973 for $200. Inflation and rising demand may shoot all these prices even higher; the opening of new smuggling networks through Mexico would tend to lower them. The fact that hospitals and pharmacies were buying the drug legally as an anesthetic for $31.50 an ounce (about a dollar a gram) in 1975 should give some idea of the risks and profits in the illicit trade.[13]

The large-scale traffic is controlled by Latin Americans, especially Colombians and Cubans, and to a lesser extent North American blacks;

white North American small-time independent dealers who consider themselves part of the counterculture are apparently being put out of business. But people in many different social circumstances are involved at one level or another. One recent arrest broke up a ring transporting the drug from Bolivia to New York that included a New York physician and the former president of a pharmaceuticals company in New Jersey. Columbia University undergraduates have been arrested for selling it, and professional football players are suspected of being involved in smuggling. A former chief of the narcotics police in Chile (1966 to 1969) was extradited to New York in 1974 for his alleged part in a cocaine smuggling operation that included four other former high Chilean drug officials who are now fugitives. Military aircraft and diplomatic pouches, which are not subject to regular customs inspection, are said to be common means of transportation. This is another indication that many members of South American governing elites are involved in the trade. Meanwhile, in August 1974, 435 North American couriers—many of them students or other tourists persuaded to try to earn a share of that easy money—were in Mexican prisons, some for marihuana or hashish smuggling, but many on cocaine charges.[14]

A particularly interesting and important element is the Cuban gangs, reported to be running most of the Miami and New York operations, which have been smuggling cocaine since the days when it was a small business instead of a big one. After Castro's revolution, exiles resumed operations in Florida. They include former Cuban government officials; one was arrested on cocaine charges in July 1973. Some of the desperadoes once trained by the CIA for what proved to be abortive invasions of Cuba are also apparently involved. A Drug Enforcement Administration official has been quoted as saying, "Cuban brigades seeking political asylum in Miami . . . most are dope peddlers. Not some, not a few. But most." [15] "Dope" here refers mainly to cocaine; the Cubans have not yet entered the heroin business to any great extent. Miami is probably the biggest center of cocaine traffic, and many small businesses in southern Florida are said to be financed by cocaine money.

The United States has been increasing its drug police force in South America, but these agents obtain insufficient cooperation from the governments and people of the countries they are assigned to. Over half of the 200 major Colombian cocaine and marihuana traffickers have been indicted in the United States, but under present treaties they cannot be extradited and they are not prosecuted at home. The $22,000,000 a year provided in grants to Latin American countries to combat the drug trade in the last few years has had limited effect. From July 1973 to May 1975,

457 cocaine traffickers were arrested and 73 laboratories destroyed, but the trade keeps growing. An apparent exception to the rule of insufficient cooperation is Chile, where an ingenious Drug Enforcement Administration official persuaded the *junta* to extradite 19 important traffickers on the admittedly spurious ground that they threatened state security because radical groups might use money from cocaine to buy arms. Shipments from Chile are estimated to have dropped from 200 kg to 11 kg a month since the expulsion.[16] Some arrests by the United States and Chilean governments suggest that cocaine charges are being used to persecute political opponents of the military regime in Chile. For example, a professor at the University of Wisconsin was acquitted on charges of cocaine smuggling in a federal district court in Brooklyn in July 1975, after contending that he was being prosecuted because he had worked in an organization to help Chilean radicals after the coup d'état.[17] Cocaine dealers in general are anything but radical, and, like Castro, other Latin American radicals are opposed to the traffic.

A United States diplomat is quoted in a 1975 *New York Times* article as saying, "These countries don't have a drug problem themselves. There's no mutual interest to work with."[18] What this means is not that South Americans do not use cocaine but that they do not regard it (or cannabis) with the horror that North American drug enforcement officials consider appropriate. It is hard for them to take the menace of cocaine seriously while the coca leaf serves as the ordinary daily drug of millions in Peru and Bolivia—even if they are poor and often despised Indians. (It is the same with opiates in Southeast Asia.) Cocaine itself has always been relatively easy to buy, too. A 1949 article in *Time* tells how it is sold openly, in spite of the laws, at market stalls in Callao, Peru. It quotes a dealer: "If you're poor, you're hungry. *Pichicato* [cocaine] fixes that. If you're rich, you want an aphrodisiac. *Pichicato* fixes that too. It's a sure cure for everything."[19] Although the drug may no longer appear quite so openly in marketplaces, reports we have heard from travelers in South America suggest that North Americans with a little money or the right friends can obtain it easily. As for the Cubans, an exile journalist in Miami told a *New York Times* reporter: "Some Cubans think that the cocaine is like the violation of the tax. But the heroin is a vice."[20] Most of the people who deal in cocaine, unlike big heroin operators and like illicit alcohol refiners, use the drug they sell. The game of evading the cocaine laws is like the game of evading income taxes commonly played in many countries, or like the methods once adopted in the United States in the face of alcohol prohibition. Cocaine traffickers, as we have seen, have government connections in Latin America, and police are easily bribed. In the circumstances, it is unlikely that narcotics officials can keep the traffic from increasing.

Cutting

A problem (and an argument for legalization) that always arises with illegal commodities is adulteration. In the 1920s no one could be sure what was in a bottle labeled whiskey; today, heroin addicts do not know the proportion of quinine or lactose (milk sugar) in their drug. Cocaine, too, is almost always cut or diluted with various inert substances or other drugs before it reaches the retail market. Many people are getting little more from their black-market cocaine than a numb palate and the social status of having sniffed it. Since dealers and police cooperate in a kind of de facto conspiracy to prevent knowledge of the kinds and quantity of adulterants from reaching the customers, it is especially hard to find information on the subject. Aspirin, boric acid, and bicarbonate of soda were mentioned as common adulterants in the 1920s. According to "Jimmy," the subject of Richard Woodley's study, cocaine could be distinguished from the synthetics benzocaine and procaine because it numbed the tongue but did not "freeze" it. He told Woodley, referring to the number of parts of sugar to each part of cocaine that the drug he bought would tolerate without losing its effect, "Best superfine dope will stand a twelve. My stuff can take a three." He actually claimed to prefer cut or "stepped on" to pure cocaine; some of our interview subjects agreed. Marc Olden estimates that the highest quality generally available on the street in New York City is 25 percent.[21]

The result is that in using cocaine people usually do not know what or how much they are taking into their bodies. "Jimmy," who buys and sells only cut cocaine himself, is quoted as saying, "Drugstore coke [i.e., pure] is so strong it'll wreck you." In Bruce Jay Friedman's novel, *About Harry Towns* (1974), the apparently autobiographical hero, if asked about the effects of cocaine, "would say it was subtle and leave it at that." But he and his friends know that less subtle stuff is available too: ". . . they would tell each other stories about coke they had either heard about or tried personally, coke that was like a blow on the head, coke that came untouched from the drug companies, coke so strong it was used in cataract eye operations." [22] One of our interview subjects told us, "Cuts can sometimes be total highs in themselves. One person I know sells a cut composed of procaine, lidocaine, caffeine, and something else. There's no coke in it. But you get a freeze from the procaine, a buzz from the lido-caine, and the caffeine keeps you going . . . that's one of the pitfalls of an illegal product." Although it is hard to tell, most cocaine users have the impression that quality has been declining as the popularity of the drug rises. As one man who had used cocaine long before it became fashion-able told us in an interview, "The reason why I curtailed, cut down, was that it wasn't *coke* any more." The use of cuts may be increasing because organized crime is becoming more involved in the traffic. The problem of quality control that plagued Freud and his predecessors has returned for entirely different reasons.

But too much of the information about cuts is only rumor, some of it put about by narcotics officials with an interest in frightening or dis-couraging the public. That is why the work of the PharmChem Research Foundation, a chemical laboratory in Palo Alto, California, that analyzes samples of street drugs, is so interesting. An administrative regulation promulgated by the Drug Enforcement Administration in mid-1974 has prevented this group from publishing quantitative data on individual samples of illicit drugs contributed by anonymous donors. The ostensible purpose is to keep dealers from using it to check on quality. But the effect is to keep everyone in the dark and make using the drugs as dangerous as possible, while dealers continue to sell whatever they have on hand. The samples analyzed by PharmChem are not necessarily typical, and they come almost exclusively from the West Coast; but they provide one of the few sources of reliable information on this important subject.

In an issue entitled "Heroin and Cocaine Adulteration," based on anal-yses made in 1973, *The PharmChem Newsletter* reported that 73 percent of the 40 samples of alleged cocaine contained cocaine as the only *drug*. Twenty-one percent also contained synthetic local anesthetics, and 6 per-cent had amphetamine, caffeine, phencyclidine, some other drug, or no drug at all. The newsletter points out that procaine, the most commonly found local anesthetic, is also the least toxic—about one-third as toxic as cocaine or lidocaine. Benzocaine is particularly dangerous if injected because it is relatively insoluble and may cause blood clots. Three percent of the samples analyzed contained it. The cocaine content of samples containing no other drug varied from 14 percent to 89 percent (pure cocaine hydrochloride), with an average of about 60 percent. Price was unrelated to purity. The most common inert adulterants were mannitol (an alcohol derived by reduction from fructose) and lactose. Later lists compiled under the new regulations can give no percentages for individual samples, but they reveal that glucose, sodium bicarbonate, and especially inositol (a member of the vitamin B-2 complex) are also being used as adulterants. In a 1974 issue the editors indicate that the average proportion of cocaine alkaloid in the samples analyzed was 65 percent when the sample contained no other drug (as was usually the case) and 39 percent when it contained other drugs. Inositol, mannitol, and lactose were the most common cuts. Nothing as dangerous as quinine, strychnine, or asbestos was found, and there were no amphetamines, either. The percentage of pure cocaine in these samples actually seems high. Maybe people who know enough to send what they have bought to the Pharm-Chem Research Foundation also have access to particularly reliable sources of drugs; maybe, as the Drug Enforcement Administration fears, some of them are dealers who have nearly pure supplies that they intend to adulterate further and sell. According to Richard Ashley, however, West Coast cocaine is purer than the drug found in the East because the local traffic has not yet been monopolized by Cuban exiles.[23]

Several methods of assaying a substance for cocaine are used in the illicit traffic. Cobalt thiocyanate is sold as part of a kit for testing the quality of illicit cocaine. It produces a blue precipitate that dissolves in hydrochloric acid; the deeper the blue, the purer the cocaine.* Another test is to drop the powder into a dark-glass jar containing sodium hypochlorite (Clorox). If it is cocaine, a white halo will appear as it drops to the bottom. If any red appears, it has been cut with a synthetic local anesthetic. Pure cocaine hydrochloride (the form in which cocaine is usually used) dissolves instantly in water and readily in methyl alcohol; any powder that does not dissolve is probably a sugar. Burned on aluminum foil, nearly pure cocaine hydrochloride produces a gray or red-brown stain; a black residue means sugar, popping sounds mean amphetamine, and sizzling means procaine; salts do not burn, but remain as a residue. Most cuts, and especially the most common ones—sugars—dull the sparkle of the crystalline powder. Sugar makes the taste sweeter, salt makes it more bitter, and synthetic local anesthetics have a stronger numbing effect.

* Drug-enforcement agents use a version of the cobalt thiocyanate method as a field test for cocaine hydrochloride. They add a 2 percent solution of cobalt thiocyanate in water, diluted in the field with glycerine, to the suspect substance. If it contains cocaine, a blue precipitate will form; concentrated hydrochloric acid will redissolve the precipitate; and chloroform will cause the blue color to reappear in the lower layer. This assay is said to distinguish cocaine from any other substance except the rare coca alkaloid tropacocaine. See "Cocaine Identification," *Drug Enforcement* 1 (Spring 1974):26–27. A recent article points out that the test is adequate for pure drugs but does not distinguish cocaine from certain mixtures of lidocaine (a synthetic local anesthetic) with other drugs; it recommends supplementary confirmation by thin-layer chromatography that the drug is an alkaloid and not a mixture of synthetic substances. See Charles I. Winek and Timothy Eastly, "Cocaine Identification," *Clinical Toxicology* 8 (1975): 205–210. For a test for cocaine in urine, see F. Fish and W. D. C. Wilson, "Gas Chromatographic Determination of Morphine and Cocaine in Urine," *Journal of Chromatography* 40 (1969): 164–168.

Methamphetamine burns the nasal passage when it is sniffed, and Epsom salts may cause diarrhea.[24]

Cocaine Use and Users

On the question of who is buying and using whatever passes for cocaine on the retail market, there are plenty of anecdotes and rumors and few quantifiable data. We begin with statistical samples, accepting their possible bias or unreliability. In 1973 the National Commission on Marihuana and Drug Abuse estimated that 4,800,000 people in the United States had used cocaine at least once, about 3.2 percent of all adults and 1.5 percent of adolescents; this was slightly higher than the number using heroin. Eighty percent of the people surveyed knew no one who had used cocaine. A 1972 survey suggested that 10.2 percent of all college students had tried it. A questionnaire distributed in 1973 to 1,629 students on the Chicago Circle and Urbana-Champaign campuses of the University of Illinois revealed that 4.6 percent of them had used cocaine, 0.8 in the preceding month. Of the main psychoactive drugs, only heroin was used less. Proportionately more blacks (8.5 percent) than whites (4.4 percent), more liberal arts majors than education, engineering, and business majors, and slightly more higher- and middle-income than lower-income students had used it. There was no significant correlation between the use of cocaine (or any other drug) and grades. A survey of over 50,000 high school students in 1971 indicated that 5 percent of them had used cocaine at least once, and 2 percent in the preceding week. About 0.6 percent had used it ten or more times. The corresponding figure for amphetamines was 3 percent, for marihuana 8 percent, for tobacco 23 percent, and for alcohol 43 percent.[25] Even so, the numbers seem too high for 1971. Some of the students must have been boasting, and others must have confused cocaine with cocoa, Coca-Cola, or other drugs.

A recent analysis by the Drug Enforcement Administration based on reports from hospital emergency rooms, inpatient units, county medical examiners and coroners, and drug crisis intervention centers provides further evidence that cocaine is not yet commonly used. The analysis covers about two dozen cities for the period July 1973 to March 1974; the data concern only drug abuse episodes that caused the person involved or someone in contact with him to seek help at one of the listed places. Cocaine alone or in combination with other drugs was mentioned 1,764 times, 1.5 percent of the total; about one-third of the cocaine episodes involved blacks, and 70 percent involved males. According to the study, perhaps half of them were caused by cocaine alone. The distribution between crisis centers (69 percent) and emergency rooms (25 percent) resembles the pattern for amphetamine (60 percent and 34 percent), LSD (69 percent and 29 percent), and marihuana (83 percent and 14 percent), as opposed to heroin (49 percent and 42 percent), phenobarbital (13 percent and 74 percent), or Valium (10 percent and 85 percent). Cocaine is twentieth on the list of drugs causing crises reported in this way. It might be suggested that the study indicates only that cocaine is relatively innocuous, not that it is rarely used. This interpretation cannot be discounted, but in any case it would not exclude the one we have made. In fact, it looks as though for most drugs the number of reported crises is related to frequency of use. Drugs that are relatively safe but commonly used appear high on the list: Valium (diazepam) is first, marihuana fifth, and aspirin seventh. Nothing is said about the *kinds* of episodes involved, but it is reasonable to assume that most of the crisis intervention center cases (for all drugs) were anxiety or panic reactions that required mainly support and reassurance rather than medical attention. Half of all mentions of cocaine came from three cities: Miami, Los Angeles, and New York.[26]

A woman we interviewed wrote an account for us of how she became involved in using cocaine. It began in the spring of 1973, when she went to work for a radio station:

I was aware that many of the people working for the same radio station were into coke, but I had to become a trusted person before I knew the extent of it. At first I was just offered coke at work, a kind of pick-me-up during the day. Or at a party someone might put some out. I considered it an act of generosity. There's no denying that whoever put out the coke became a bit more prestigious to those who were snorting it up. I found myself attracted to people who had coke. I can even say I formed friendships on that basis. There was something nice in sneaking into the bathroom or a closet at the station, snorting some coke with a friend, coming out high and together with our secret. After snorting coke I came back to my work with a freshness and vitality that I enjoyed. Considering the long hours I put into preparing news stories, writing and producing them in the studio, coke became an aid I counted on. Three months or so after I started using it, it became evident that I could not rely on being offered coke. I wanted to have it accessible to me. So I considered buying some. I also felt that it was my turn to lay out some coke to the friends who had given me some, and I wanted that element of distinction.

It was not difficult finding someone to buy coke from since others who worked at the station had formed a kind of cooperative coke pool. One person bought quantity, a couple of ounces, and then sold it to us for the price he got it for. He made a gram selling it and we were able to get good quality coke (75 percent or more) for what was then a reasonable price—$55 to $65 a gram.

The same woman told us, "Cocaine is something you expect to see at promotion parties; it has become almost a way of payment. . . . Musicians expect to get it before a concert. They come into town and the first thing their road managers do is try to locate a source of cocaine. . . . People stuck in a job that's forcing them to put out a lot of energy, cocaine is getting them through." Although there are no surveys that provide a reliable indication of who uses cocaine, clearly workers in high-pressure elite environments of this kind—the entertainment business, radio and television, advertising, and so on—are most heavily involved. It is unusual, for example, to leaf through a couple of issues of a so-called underground newspaper or a publication devoted to popular music without finding several casual references to cocaine. According to *Rolling Stone* magazine, "Already it is responsible for wasting a number of top musical names." One singer calls it a "temporary cure-all." Another refers to it as "vitamin C" and uses it in the same quantities that others use the real vitamin C. Rock songs make open references to it; the musicians and their entourages use it for rehearsals and performances as well as at parties. Several rock stars are supposed to have refused to attack cocaine on television because it would be hypocritical; they were more willing to warn against amphetamines and barbiturates. Occasionally, the situation is publicly acknowledged for one reason or another. For example, a member of the rock group Grateful Dead was arrested for possession of cocaine in 1973. And during one of the periodic scandals in the recording business it transpired that an assistant to the president of Columbia records was regularly buying $100 worth of cocaine for visiting musicians and writing it off as a business expense; he declared that the drug was part of the ordinary "lifestyle" of the pop music world. Nicholas von Hoffman, in an article entitled "The Cocaine Culture: New Wave for the Rich and Hip," reports that when one rock musician last went on tour, "one of the members of his astonishing, rocking, rolling, and rollicking entourage was paid $20,000 to do nothing but the holding. He was given extra money, maybe another $20,000, to score the cocaine, but his main job was to take the fall in case of a bust." According to von Hoffman, "There are people around here [Los Angeles] who'll tell you that Mr. Kung Fu, Bruce Lee, died of overcoking, that it is wrecking music, if not the industry: 'The drug culture has lost its taste buds. They assault you. Help! I've just been mugged by a hit record.' " [27]
Other places where cocaine dealing has come to the attention of the

press through arrests or scandal are the Columbia and Indiana University campuses, a Via Veneto nightclub, and an apartment in a fashionable district of London. After a cocaine arrest at the Playboy mansion in Chicago, Hugh Hefner was investigated (and cleared) by the DEA on charges of distributing the drug. In 1974 the DEA broke up a distribution ring in Aspen, Colorado, in a project humorously designated "Operation Snowflake." The conjunction of high altitude, high life, and vigorous physical exercise occurring at fashionable ski resorts appears to make them an ideal geographical and cultural setting for cocaine.[28]

In the 1920s Joël and Fränkel described the group of cocaine users in each city as a kind of secret society with its own meeting places, jargon, poetry, and songs. However it was then in Europe, now in America the secret is open, and there is no cocaine set, apart from the various smart and jet sets who indulge in the drug. Most of the people whose lives revolve around cocaine are those who make their living from it. But the cocaine scene can sometimes be identified by physical as well as sociological location. Von Hoffman quotes a Los Angeles record producer: "There are certain clubs in this town where you feel out of place if you aren't wired to the teeth. Whole clubs are based on being wired. Even the waitresses are wired. That fast cocaine tempo. You feel you've got to eat, drink, and get out of the place in an hour." [29] In any case, cocaine is still largely restricted to groups that are privileged or socially marginal or both. Outside of these circles it is known more by reputation and occasional encounters than by intimate acquaintance.

Snob appeal is important in the spread of cocaine use. It may be inducing people to pay $100 a gram for a substance that is often largely sugar. The high cost of cocaine and its powerful reputation as an elite drug tend to persuade people that it is desirable. It is an ideal mode of conspicuous consumption. As von Hoffman puts it, "It has come home to you that you can buy anything and do anything, and you've got to do it. How do you solve your problem? You get into cocaine." As one man we interviewed said, "I felt I'd better enjoy the experience because it was so hard to get hold of." Marc Olden quotes a rock musician on his reasons for using the drug: "Getting high, getting laid, getting a lot of work done, being up and being 'on,' being strong, being creative and superaware, being hip and being 'in.' " [30] Being hip and being "in" are probably not the least of these. Buying cocaine is like buying expensive cosmetics: the outlay is partly for glamour and romance. Cocaine is called icing drug, stardust, gold dust, rich man's drug, pimp's drug, and by one wit "the thinking man's Dristan." To wear a T-shirt imprinted with the legend "Things Go Better with Coke" or "It's the Real Thing," or to carry a gold snuff spoon around one's neck is (or was until recently) to advertise membership in an elite club. "Cocaine is a luxury, it's not a lifestyle," a man we interviewed told us. But for anyone who can afford to buy it continually or knows how to obtain it from people who can, this luxury, like others, may easily become an essential part of a certain way of living. As cocaine invests this way of living with its psychopharmacological qualities, the way of living in turn affects the perception of what cocaine is—its social definition.

Nothing provides better proof of cocaine's new social status than its reappearance as a topic of public reference in the media of popular culture. Several national magazines, including *Playboy* and the *New York Times Magazine,* have carried articles about it in the last few years. The films *Easy Rider* and *Superfly,* in which the heroes were cocaine dealers, have helped to make the drug's reputation among, respectively, white cultural rebels and young blacks. (In *Easy Rider* the Mexican who sells the drug to the heroes declares, "It is life.") Robert Woodley's book-length portrayal of a Harlem cocaine dealer (*Dealer: Portrait of a Cocaine Merchant*) appeared in 1971; a novel that devotes much attention to its hero's dealings with and ambivalent attitudes toward cocaine (*About Harry Towns,* by Bruce Jay Friedman) was published in 1974. The black comedian Richard Pryor, formerly a heavy cocaine user, has a recorded comedy routine about the drug and its effects ("He told me, 'It's not habit forming. I've been using it every day for 15 years and I don't have a habit.' ") Cocaine has also been conspicuous as an inspiration for the lyrics of popular songs. In the 1920s there was a "Ballad of Cocaine Lil" and also a song about a man who shot his woman while high on cocaine. Huddie Ledbetter ("Leadbelly") wrote a song recorded in 1933 called "Take a Whiff on Me":

> *Whiffaree and whiffarye*
> *Gonna keep on whiffing till I die*
> *An' ho, ho, baby, take a whiff on me.*
>
> *Cocaine for horses an' not for men.*
> *Doctors say it kill you but they don't say when.*
> *An' ho, ho, baby, take a whiff on me.*

Dave Van Ronk's "Cocaine Blues" runs, in part, "Come here mama/ Come here quick/ This old cocaine/ 'bout to make me sick./ Cocaine, cocaine/ running around my brain." Another balladeer, Hoyt Axton, sings of a friend buying a "one-way ticket" to heaven on "an airline made of snow" and ultimately "Flyin' low/ dyin' slow/ blinded by snow." The ideal large-scale cocaine consumer, for financial, professional, and cultural reasons, is a rock musician; the lyrics of rock songs have been attesting to familiarity with the drug since the mid-1960s. Richard Ashley cites references by Laura Nyro in 1967 (it's even better to get off the "poverty train" than get high on "sweet cocaine"), by the Rolling Stones in 1970 ("And there will always be a space in my parking lot/ when you need a little coke and sympathy," from "Let It Bleed"), the Grateful Dead, also in 1970 ("Driving that train/High on cocaine/ Casey Jones you'd better/ watch your speed," from "Casey Jones"), the Jefferson Airplane in 1971 ("Earth Mother your children are here/ high and feeling dandy/ Earth Mother your children are here/ ripped on coke and candy"), and the Stones again in 1971 ("Sweet cousin cocaine laid his cool, cool hands on my head," from "Sister Morphine").[31] A hit song recorded in 1975 by Ringo Star, the former Beatle, is less laudatory; its doggerel concerns a series of drugs, including cocaine, that the singer has given up because he is "tired of waking up on the floor."

Today cocaine—also known as coke, snow, flake, blow, leaf, medicine, candy, happy dust, freeze, C, Carrie, Dama Blanca, lady, and girl (heroin is "boy")—is usually taken through a process of vigorous sniffing called snorting or blowing. It is more powerful injected under the skin or intravenously, but this method seemed to be largely confined to heroin addicts; most people find it more difficult to overcome the barrier against using hypodermic needles than to overcome the barrier against using illicit drugs. Today cocaine is rarely eaten or drunk, as in the days of Mariani's wine, because for most users the mild stimulation does not justify the high price. Since it is absorbed through mucous membranes anywhere in the body, it can also be applied to the genitals—a method that may produce some tingling caused by partial local anesthesia but is otherwise valued more for its symbolic licentiousness than for any strengthening of the drug effect. Cocaine is usually chopped up with a safety razor and sniffed from a measuring spoon, a soda straw, or a tightly rolled cigarette paper or dollar bill (higher denominations for those who want to display their wealth). But recently there has been a proliferation of expensive accessories that confirm and promote its *premier cru* status among illicit drugs. Advertisements can be found for "shotgun spoons" ($6), gold-capped safety razors ($30), gold straws ($75), gold-jacketed glass storage bottles ($200), mirrors and jade blocks for chopping, spring-loaded snorting devices or "toots," and an elaborate "dessert service tray" ($69), pictured with a glass of liqueur.[32] Everything suggests that cocaine is becoming one of the routine luxuries provided by our consumer society.

The Future

The most significant sociological fact about cocaine today is that it is rapidly attaining unofficial respectability in the same way as marihuana in the 1960s. It is accepted as a relatively innocuous stimulant, casually used by those who can afford it to brighten the day or the evening. Several serious books and articles on it have appeared in the last few years, none of them displaying the kind of horror that was once standard in the literature. Use of cocaine is gradually spreading in the upper middle class. College students, young professional men and women, and middle-class radicals have begun to experiment with it. A new elite mainstream has been created by the convergence of the old Hollywood-Broadway, black, and Latin cultural practices and the drug culture of the 1960s; the present status of cocaine is both a product of this convergence and the perfect symbol of it. A glance at *High Times* magazine, the highly successful new publication that serves as the *Playboy* of the drug culture, reveals that cocaine is placed on a par with marihuana as a pleasure drug and accorded none of the ambivalence or distrust associated with alcohol, amphetamines, and barbiturates or the somewhat awed respect reserved for psychedelics. Given the price of illicit cocaine, this implies that *High Times,* in spite of its vague gestures of radicalism and its necessary opposition to the activities of the drug police, does not represent anything like a counterculture; no unworldly hippie is going to buy the expensive cocaine-sniffing apparatus advertised in its pages. The cocaine situation is symbolic of the death of the counterculture, to the extent that it was more than a creation of the mass media (underground *and* orthodox)—or at least it constitutes a sign that the counterculture has been absorbed into American society as a whole, the former adversary relationship between the two reduced to the practical issue of skirmishes with the law.

Whether the unofficial acceptability of cocaine to an increasingly large section of the middle class can be translated into official respectability is doubtful, but there are bound to be some changes. Once the drug was used mainly by the rich and privileged, who were sheltered from the law and public disapproval, or by blacks, small-time criminals, and others who had no resources for public opposition. But now the kind of person who is both a potential victim and a potential manipulator of the legal machinery has arrived on the scene. These people are articulate and have access to legal skills and sources of publicity; for example, a 1974 article in the *New York Times Magazine* was practically an endorsement of cocaine.[33] The new cocaine users are often veterans of the cultural civil war of the 1960s and conscious of the irrationality of our drug laws and policies. They not only know what they want but have ideologues, social philosophers, or gurus to tell them why they should want it. Some victories have already been won in the marihuana campaigns, and now, with the help of public defenders, radical law firms, and affidavits from prominent physicians and psychiatrists, the cocaine issue is being brought to attention.

The most celebrated case of this kind is the arrest of the radical leader Abbie Hoffman in 1973 for selling cocaine to police in New York City, but there have been several other similar legal actions. We have examined briefs and affidavits from some of these cases, and they all follow the same pattern. Apparently the first step in making a drug respectable, for radicals and cultural rebels as well as for physicians, police, and government officials, is to establish that it is not an opiate, is not like the opiates, is not a steppingstone to the opiates, and is not for the most part used by the same people who use opiates. As we shall explain under "A Note on Cocaine and Opiates," at the end of Chapter 6, this devil theory of heroin and morphine is misleading. Nevertheless, the approach is very effective and sensible, not only because most people believe the theory but also because laws that classify cocaine as a narcotic along with the opiates are particularly irrational and therefore subject to Constitutional challenge on due process and equal protection grounds. The legal briefs and affidavits we have read properly point out that cocaine should be classed with amphetamines as a stimulant and also insist that it is actually not so dangerous as amphetamines, alcohol, barbiturates, and other less restricted drugs.

The immediate effect of legal challenges is likely to be educational: judges may learn to mete out more lenient punishments whenever they are not required by statute to impose absurdly harsh ones. But, as the difficulties encountered in the struggle to reform the laws on marihuana or sexual activity show, nothing moves more glacially than official attitudes toward punitive statutes based on a formerly entrenched popular prejudice—even when the men who make and enforce the laws no longer really believe in them. Nevertheless, there are already signs of change, at least at the level of government commissions that operate at some distance from the effects of popular prejudice. In September 1975 a group consisting of representatives of 11 federal departments and agencies concerned with drugs presented to President Ford a White Paper on drug abuse which classifies cocaine as a minor problem compared to all other illicit pleasure drugs except marihuana, much less serious than barbiturates, amphetamines, and heroin. They add the reservation that cocaine might become a bigger problem if it were used more extensively, but they conclude that drug-enforcement officials should devote less attention and resources to it—for example, working more often in Mexico, where heroin is being smuggled, and less often in Miami, where they are more likely to find only cocaine or marihuana.[34] The recommendations of presidential commissions are often considered radical and not put into effect until long after they are made, if ever. But in this case President Ford has actually issued a general endorsement of the White Paper's conclusions in a statement for the press.[35] How soon this change in attitude will be translated into action remains in doubt. If the number of cocaine arrests rises to the level already reached by marihuana arrests (according to the Federal Bureau of Investigation, there were 445,000 arrests for marihuana in 1974 and only 101,000 arrests for cocaine and opium derivatives together), the strain on government time and financial resources may become so great that serious policy changes will be necessary. But the chances are against substantial change in the laws themselves in the near future; even if statutes declaring cocaine to be a narcotic were voided as unconstitutional, they could be reenacted with the same penalties but with the offending terminology removed. At most, the prospects are for an attenuation but not a cessation of hostilities, on the pattern supplied by the recent history of marihuana.

Price is now the biggest obstacle to a higher level of cocaine consumption. It depends to some extent on the operations of drug-enforcement agents, but also on the efficiency of the refining and smuggling network, and, of course, on the level of demand. In spite of the increased supply in recent years, the cost of cocaine has been rising fast and the quality declining. If the economic recession deepens, cocaine use may decline as it did in the Depression of the 1930s. It is also possible that South American governments will become serious about suppressing the traffic. There are no signs of this right now, in spite of the draconian penalties occasionally imposed on individual cocaine dealers and some pretense of coordinating antidrug operations at the request of the United States government; cocaine is too much a part of the social fabric in Latin America and too useful in too many ways, especially as a source of income for corrupt officials and a means of prosecuting those whom they consider undesirable for one reason or another. But truly revolutionary governments with puritan ideas about drugs might effectively suppress the cocaine traffic, which is associated with decadent high life among the old ruling class; that is what Castro apparently did in Cuba. If that ever happened, and if the coca fields of Peru and Bolivia were destroyed, as the United Nations demands, cultivation would have to be resumed somewhere else in the tropics where no mass demand in the form of a traditional coca-chewing population exists. At the moment, there is no prospect of laboratory synthesis on a commercial scale. Meanwhile, however, new smuggling networks are being opened, and the demand is rising. So many variables are involved that it is hard to predict the future of cocaine as a pleasure drug.

PART II

4

FROM PLANT
TO INTOXICANT

Botany and Cultivation

Coca is cultivated principally in warm valleys on the eastern slope of
the Andes, at altitudes of 1,500 to 6,000 feet. The region of cultivation extends from Colombia in the north to the Cochabamba region of Bolivia in
the south and eastward into the Amazon basin. Some coca is also grown
on the Pacific slope of the Andes in Peru. In the past, it was also grown
commercially in British Guiana, Jamaica, Madagascar, the Cameroons,
India, Ceylon, and especially Java. For best yields the shrub requires con-
tinuous high humidity and a uniform mean temperature of about 65°F
throughout the year. Frost kills plants grown at high altitudes, and the
excessive heat of the Amazon lowlands apparently lowers the content of
cocaine and related compounds. The plant needs a soil free of limestone
and thrives in the red clay of the tropical Andes, often on land that is too
poor for other crops.

The domesticated species of coca are identified botanically as members
of the family Erythroxylaceae and the genus *Erythroxylum* (sometimes
written *Erythroxylon*).* Otherwise their classification is somewhat un-

---

* Patrick Browne first described the genus in 1756 and gave it the name *Erythroxylum*. But most bot-
anists doubted that his description was technically adequate and therefore accepted instead the form
Erythroxylon used by Linnaeus when he redescribed the genus in 1759. The consensus is now shifting
back to recognition of Browne's priority and the name *Erythroxylum*.

certain. It appears that one species, *E. coca,* predominates in the Amazon basin, in Bolivia, and in most parts of Peru. Two variants of another species, *E. novogranatense* (after "Nueva Granada," the old Spanish name for Colombia), are also cultivated, one in Colombia and the other on the Pacific slope of the Andes in Peru. *E. novogranatense* was once grown more extensively throughout the Caribbean and, more recently, in Java and Ceylon. Further research now being conducted on the taxonomy of the genus *Erythroxylum* may modify these species designations and also identify the wild ancestors of the cultivated forms of coca.

In Peru and Bolivia, *cocales,* or coca farms, cover whole terraced mountainsides. Some are large plantations; others are small family holdings farmed by Indians. The basic methods of cultivation have been the same for hundreds of years. In a nursery with a thatched roof, young plants are started from seed or from cuttings. After six months or a year, when they are about 18 inches high, they are set out in rows separated by small earthen walls. After five years the shrub reaches full height, 12 feet, or higher in some varieties; it is usually pruned back to six to nine feet for convenience in harvesting. The coca plant produces a creamy white flower with tonguelike appendages on the petal, and it forms a deep red, small, egg-shaped fruit with a pit. The fruit is used only for seeds; it is the leaves that are harvested. They vary considerably in size and shape but tend to be oval, about an inch or two long and half an inch wide. They are considered mature when they are faintly yellow or when they tend to break off in response to bending. At this stage, which is achieved about a year or 18 months after sowing, the first harvest (*quita calzón,* or "taking off the underpants") begins; it is more a trimming than a harvest. Thereafter the leaves are harvested three or four times a year. The regular harvests (*mittas*) have traditional seasonal names, less often used today: *mitta de marzo* in spring; *mitta de San Juan* at the festival of St. John, late in June; and *mitta de Todos Santos,* the All Saints' harvest, in October or November.

The leaves are picked, often by families working together, emptied into sacks, and conveyed to drying sheds that open into closed courts. There they are spread in thin layers on a slate or concrete pavement, or on the ground, and dried in the sun. (Coca that has dried fast is known as *coca del día* and commands a high price.) The crisp leaves are now thrown in a heap for several days to absorb moisture from the air so that they will not be too brittle to pack. Then they are dried in the sun for another half hour and packed. The well-cured leaf is olive green, pliable, clean, smooth, and slightly glossy; it retains some moisture and the subtle coca aroma, which resembles new-mown hay. According to Mortimer, the leaf can be preserved for several years if it is properly stored and handled. He estimates that each bush produces four ounces of fresh leaves or 1.6 ounces of dried leaves at each harvest and that the bushes are planted 7,000 to the acre. With three harvests a year, that means 2,200 pounds of dried leaves per acre each year. The leaves are commonly packed for shipping in bales that weigh 20 to 25 pounds and then transported—formerly by mule or llama, now by truck—to the point of sale.[1]

Chemistry and Extraction

Cocaine is one of the group of alkaloids, substances occurring naturally in plants. Alkaloids are basic (alkaline) compounds synthesized by living organisms from amino acids; they have a closed carbon ring that contains nitrogen and are pharmacologically active in animals and man. Some examples are caffeine, from the coffee and other plants; morphine and codeine, from the opium poppy; quinine, from cinchona bark; strychnine, from *Nux vomica;* and nicotine, from tobacco. The term is used somewhat loosely; for example, substances lacking some of the defining characteristics may be called alkaloids if they are pharmacologically active and their distribution in nature is restricted to a few plants; a compound like the B vitamin thiamine is not usually classified as an alkaloid simply because its distribution is nearly universal. Some compounds that do not have the correct ring structure, like mescaline, the derivative of the peyote cactus, may be called either protoalkaloids or alkaloids.

The alkaloids of *Erythroxylum coca* belong to six closely related groups: 1) cocaine and some variants, including cinnamylcocaine and truxillines; 2) methylecgonine and methylecgonidine; 3) benzoylecgonine; 4) tropeines, e.g., tropacocaine; 5) dihydroxytropane; 6) hygrines, including hygrine, beta-hygrine, cuscohygrine, and hygroline. From 50 to 90 percent of the alkaloid content of the coca leaf is cocaine. Leaves from *E. novogranatense* are richer in alkaloids than *E. coca*— about 2 percent by weight as opposed to 0.5–1 percent—but the latter has a greater proportion of cocaine to other alkaloids.[2] Cocaine, like several other coca alkaloids, is a tropane, chemically related to the psychoactive tropane alkaloids produced by plants of the Solanaceae family, which includes belladonna, or deadly nightshade; henbane; jimsonweed, or thorn apple (*Datura stramonium*); and mandrake. Although these drugs—atropine, hyoscyamine, and scopolamine (hyoscine)—resemble

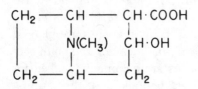 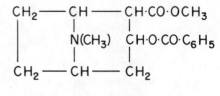

ECGONINE   COCAINE

FIGURE I
*Structural formulas of ecgonine and
its methylbenzoyl derivative, cocaine.*

cocaine structurally, their pharmacological mode of action and observed effects are quite different.

Chemically, cocaine is designated as 2-beta-carbomethoxy-3-beta-benzoxytropane. It is also described as the benzoyl ester of methylecgonine. Pure cocaine, or cocaine base, is a colorless, odorless transparent crystalline substance, almost insoluble in water and freely soluble in ether. It also dissolves in dilute acids, forming salts that are soluble in water and therefore more commonly used in medicine and recreation than cocaine base itself. Cocaine hydrochloride, also a transparent crystalline substance, is by far the most popular of these salts; it is 89 percent cocaine by weight. Both cocaine base and the hydrochloride are normally chopped into a white powder for use. Cocaine hydrochloride must be kept in a closed container or the water in the air will dissolve it, but it is resistant to the effects of sunlight and room temperature heat. Cuts do not have any effect on the potency of the remaining cocaine; but on one account, cocaine can be decomposed by molds, and the presence of sugars might enhance that process.[3]

There are several methods for obtaining refined cocaine hydrochloride on a large scale, some of them commercial secrets, but they are all variations on two patterns: extraction directly from the leaf, or semisynthetic production from ecgonine (more precisely, methylecgonine), another coca alkaloid. Crude cocaine or coca paste, called *masa* in Peru, is a mixture of alkaloids that is about two-thirds cocaine. It is produced by dissolving dried leaves in sulfuric acid and precipitating the alkaloids with sodium carbonate. A dull white or brownish powder with a sweet smell, it is sometimes smoked in pipes with marihuana. In the direct extraction process, coca paste is converted to "rock" cocaine by solution in hydrochloric acid and further treatment to remove the other alkaloids. This is the form of cocaine hydrochloride usually sold in the illicit traffic. Production of pharmaceutical-quality, or crystalline, cocaine, popularly known as "flake," requires repeated further purification. One technique employs petroleum ether, methanol, and hydrochloric acid; another employs a mixture of acetone and benzene. The semisynthetic process was commonly used before World War II with coca leaves from Java that contained a relatively small proportion of cocaine. The mixed coca alkaloids are converted to ecgonine, and cocaine hydrochloride is generated by the addition of methanol and benzoyl chloride. Direct synthesis of cocaine, without recourse to the coca leaf, is a lengthy and difficult process. Willstätter first achieved it in 1902, but neither his original method nor others introduced later have so far proved commercially practical even at the present inflated price.[4]

Unlike amphetamine and opium, for which many congeners have been synthesized and manufactured, cocaine has comparatively few analogues and substitutes with similar psychopharmacological effects. One of the other natural coca alkaloids, tropacocaine, has anesthetic and stimulant properties, and it may be chemically more accessible to structural modification. Cocaine diethylamide, a synthetic derivative, related to cocaine as LSD is related to lysergic acid, is about four times more powerful as a stimulant in mice and rabbits than cocaine itself.[5] Other alterations of the cocaine molecule to yield compounds that retain the stimulant effect would be useful to experimenters.

Pharmacology

When cocaine first came into use in the late nineteenth century, experimental pharmacology was in its beginnings and ideas about drug action and the nervous system were uncertain. Freud discussed the theory that cocaine is a "source of savings," an agent enabling the body to make more efficient use of energy and so to survive with less food. Experiments by Moreno y Maíz, von Anrep, Gazeau, and others had shown, he said, that animals given cocaine succumbed to starvation just as fast as or even faster than control animals. But he pointed out that a historical "experiment," the use of coca in the siege of La Paz in 1774 as described by Unánue, suggested the contrary. Freud concluded that the savings theory was probably false, but that "the human nervous system has an undoubted, if somewhat obscure, influence on the nourishment of tissues; psychological factors can, after all, cause a healthy man to lose weight." Freud at least understood how little he knew. Mortimer, more than ten years later, maintained that coca frees the blood from uric acid and enables it to repair tissue more effectively: "Coca simply makes better blood and healthy blood makes healthy tissue." He also thought that cocaine might diminish the consumption of carbohydrates by the muscles during exertion and so economize on oxygen.[6] The unlimited possibilities that seem to exist when there are no generally accepted models of drug action create conditions in which the idea of a wonder drug or panacea thrives.

Although there are still many mysteries in neurophysiology and neuropharmacology, we now know enough to describe the mechanism of cocaine's effect with more plausibility and precision. It has two principal actions; either may be made to predominate by varying the dose and method of application. Cocaine produces anesthesia at the site of application, and this is often the most obvious effect when it is applied to the skin or mucous membranes. Swallowed, inhaled, or injected, it enters the nervous system from the bloodstream and produces the pleasant stimulation that makes it a recreational drug. The local anesthesia is a result of its capacity, at relatively high concentrations, to block the conduction of electrical impulses within nerve cells. The stimulant effect, apparent at much lower concentrations, is achieved by interference with communication between nerve cells; cocaine does this by modifying the chemical signals passed through the synapse or neural junction. At the synapse, the electrical impulse generated in a nerve cell causes the release of a transmitter substance that diffuses across a short space to a receptor site on the adjoining cell and generates another electrical impulse; in this way signals are broadcast through a nerve network. The signal-carrying chemicals, called neurotransmitters or neurohormones, are different in different parts of the nervous system; the distinctive powers of a drug like cocaine therefore depend on the kind of neurotransmitter it affects.

Cocaine acts mainly on norepinephrine (also called noradrenalin), a neurotransmitter found in both the central nervous system (the brain and spinal cord) and the peripheral nervous system, which carries messages in the body outside of the brain. Most central and peripheral nerve cells that use norepinephrine are associated with the sympathetic nervous system, which is part of the network governing involuntary functions—muscles and glands that normally operate independently of one's intentions. Its general purpose is to put the body onto an emergency basis for coping rapidly with environmental changes. Activity of the sympathetic system produces the bodily reactions characteristic of emotional excitement, especially fear and anger; it mobilizes the organism for flight, defense, or aggression. Specific physiological effects include dilation of the pupils, increased heart rate, higher blood pressure, constriction of blood vessels in the skin and mucous membranes, increased blood sugar, rise in body temperature, and inhibition of the digestive process with increased tone of the sphincter muscles; these are all largely ways of preparing for sudden physical and mental exertion. The hormone epinephrine (adrenalin), released by the adrenal glands in times of stress, is a close chemical relative of norepinephrine and reinforces its effects. Because cocaine augments the effect of norepinephrine and therefore activates the sympathetic system, it is described as a sympathomimetic drug.

Another network governing involuntary functions is the parasympathetic nervous system, which generally produces physiological effects opposite to those of the sympathetic system: it narrows the pupils, slows the heart, lowers blood pressure, stimulates digestion, relaxes the sphincters, and so on. The transmitter substance in these nerves is acetylcholine, which is chemically unlike norepinephrine; cocaine affects parasympathetic nerves only indirectly, when they respond to sympathetic activity.

The interest in cocaine as a recreational drug derives not from its effect on such organs as the heart and digestive tract but from its direct action on the central nervous system (CNS), and in particular on its most important part, the brain. It has proved difficult to identify and locate the neurotransmitters used by the brain because of its complexity and relative inaccessibility for delicate chemical manipulation. Nevertheless, it is generally agreed that about 1 or 2 percent of CNS neurons (nerve cells) use either norepinephrine or dopamine, a related substance, as a transmitter. Dopamine is also the biosynthetic precursor of norepinephrine; that is, the body normally synthesizes norepinephrine by a chemical transformation of dopamine. Both substances belong to a class of compounds called catecholamines that also includes epinephrine; cocaine seems to augment the effect of catecholamines in the CNS just as it does in peripheral nerves.

The neurons that use catecholamines as transmitters are concentrated in a few specific areas of the brain, most of them functionally related to the sympathetic cells of the periphery. Norepinephrine is found in the hypothalamus, which regulates appetite, thirst, body temperature, sleep, and sexual arousal, as well as orchestrating anger, fear, and other emotional responses. One region of the hypothalamus, the median forebrain bundle, contains areas where electrical stimulation produces a sensation of pleasure. Norepinephrine is also an important neurotransmitter in the ascending reticular activating system (RAS), which controls mechanisms of arousal and attention. External stimuli normally reach consciousness only through the RAS, and when it is inactive the organism is asleep. Norepinephrine is also used in nerve pathways leading from the hypothalamus and RAS to the cerebellum, which controls fine motor coordination, and the cerebral cortex, which governs higher mental activity like concept formation and memory. Dopamine is found in the corpus striatum, which is part of the network governing motor functions, and also in the region of the hypothalamus regulating appetite and thirst.

Cocaine is only one of several drugs classified as stimulants that exert their influence by modifying catecholamine transmission in the CNS; caffeine and the amphetamines are others. The precise mechanism by which cocaine acts is uncertain, although there are several plausible theories. One way a stimulant effect can be produced is by preventing normal destruction or inactivation of the neurotransmitter after it has carried its message at the synapse. In most nerve cells, including all those that use catecholamines, the major inactivation process is reuptake: the neurotransmitter is partially reabsorbed by the nerve cell that released it and held in storage, so that it need not be continually resynthesized at the same rate that it is used. A commonly accepted theory is that cocaine acts primarily by blocking reuptake of catecholamines, leaving an excess of the neurotransmitter in the synapse to stimulate receptors. Imipramine and other drugs used in treating depressed patients apparently work in this way. But some experiments suggest that cocaine has no more effect on the rate of norepinephrine inactivation than procaine (Novocain), a local anesthetic without any stimulant effect; if that is so, the stimulant power of cocaine cannot be attributed solely to its effect on reuptake.[7]

A stimulant may also work by displacing neurotransmitters from their storage pools in the nerve terminal and provoking their release. Amphetamines almost certainly do this; cocaine probably does not. The effect can be demonstrated by preventing normal synthesis of catecholamines and therefore artificially depleting neurohormone stores. A substance that does this is AMPT (alpha-methyl-para-tyrosine); if animals are pretreated with AMPT and then given amphetamines, the usual amphetamine effects are not observed because there is too little of the neurohormone left to be released. By contrast, cocaine effects, in some experiments, seem to be diminished but not eliminated; this suggests that cocaine does not work predominantly by forcing release of stored catecholamines. But such conclusions are problematic because the experiments are often hard to interpret; for example, in order to release a neurotransmitter, the drug may also have to block reuptake, since it takes over the uptake mechanism to gain access to the storage pools.[8]

Because it is difficult to explain the effect of cocaine fully by release of catecholamines or reuptake blockade, some researchers now favor the theory that it acts primarily by heightening the sensitivity of the receptor sites that combine with catecholamines in nerve cells receiving their chemical message. If (as the experiments with AMPT suggest) cocaine can be active even when very small quantities of neurotransmitter are present, this hypothesis has some support. According to one version of the theory, cocaine does not act directly at the receptor site where catecholamines generate the nerve impulse but rather at nearby sites; its effect is to change the shape of the receptor molecule so that the neurohormone is more likely to generate a signal. The process is known as allosteric interaction.[9] One reason for suggesting that cocaine acts in this indirect fashion is that, unlike amphetamines, it bears little molecular resemblance to the catecholamines; this may also be the reason why it does not displace catecholamines from nerve storage pools.

There is also evidence that cocaine does not affect the transmission of dopamine, as opposed to norepinephrine, so strongly as amphetamines. For example, the drug haloperidol, which blocks receptor sites for dopamine, but not norepinephrine, seems to reduce the effect of amphetamine more than that of cocaine. (Chlorpromazine, which blocks both dopamine and norepinephrine receptor sites, affects cocaine and amphetamine in the same way).[10] Either of these stimulants may cause in animals a kind of stereotyped motion—repetitive head turning, gnawing, sniffing, and so on—which is probably controlled by dopamine-using nerve cells in the corpus striatum. But it takes much higher doses of cocaine to produce such behavior. In one recent experiment injections of cocaine even in doses as high as 10 mg per kg of body weight (the equivalent of 700 mg in a 150-pound man) caused no stereotyped behavior in rats, although amphetamine began to produce the effect at less than 1 mg per kg. It is possible that amphetamines are more active than cocaine at dopamine synapses because they actually release the neurotransmitter from storage sites, while cocaine only blocks its reuptake or makes receptor sites more sensitive.[11]

This apparent difference between cocaine and at least some of the amphetamine compounds is significant for two reasons. First, it suggests an explanation of why cocaine is somewhat different in its subjective effects from amphetamines (as we will see) and apparently tolerable and desirable at higher doses. In experiments on rats, injections of cocaine in doses up to 10 mg per kg increased the rate at which they stimulated themselves by means of electrodes placed in the median forebrain bundle (pleasure center) of the hypothalamus. Amphetamine increased the rate of self-stimulation most at .63 mg per kg and actually depressed it at higher doses as stereotyped behavior became more prominent.[12] The release of dopamine was apparently interfering with or superseding the effect of the norepinephrine-using nerve cells in the pleasure center. A second reason why differences between norepinephrine and dopamine effects are so important is that dopamine mechanisms may be the cause of the "model psychosis" produced by both cocaine and amphetamines, but more often by amphetamines. We will eventually discuss these matters in more detail.

A reasonable conclusion is that cocaine affects the nervous system in somewhat the same way as amphetamines, but with subtle differences that may turn out to be significant. It would be particularly useful for any hypothesis to account for an important difference between the organism's response to cocaine and its response to amphetamines, which we discuss more fully later: that amphetamines often produce tolerance, and cocaine apparently does not. Needless to say, no theory has been able to fully explain this or other unique features of the pharmacology of cocaine.*

Detailed information on the processes by which the body alters, inactivates, and eliminates cocaine is lacking, but some facts are known. Recently a study of monkeys receiving cocaine by injection showed that after half an hour about one-quarter of the drug is found in the brain as norcocaine, a breakdown product which blocks reuptake of norepinephrine in the test tube and may be active in the living brain as well. Eventually cocaine is inactivated when it is broken down by enzymes in either the bloodstream or the liver, where it is converted to the related alkaloids ecgonine and benzoylecgonine; the liver can detoxify the equivalent of one lethal dose an hour. Some of the cocaine absorbed by the body is also excreted unchanged in the urine. Various studies have reported values ranging from 0.5 percent to 21 percent; in one case of overdose, as high as 54 percent. Studies on coca chewers showed that about

---

* Amphetamines and cocaine both produce anorexia (loss of appetite), presumably by interfering with appetite regulation in the hypothalamus. Amphetamine anorexia, like other amphetamine effects, is nullified by AMPT (see, for example, A. Groppetti, "Amphetamines and Cocaine on Amine Turnover," *Life Sciences* 13 [1973]: lxii–lxiii). If cocaine anorexia is less affected by AMPT, it too may be caused by heightening of receptor sensitivity rather than release of catecholamines. Tolerance to amphetamine anorexia notoriously develops rather quickly (see, for example, Lester Grinspoon and Peter Hedblom, *The Speed Culture: Amphetamine Use and Abuse in America* [Cambridge: Harvard University Press, 1975], pp. 210–211). If cocaine anorexia has a different mechanism, tolerance to it may arise much less easily and cocaine may be a more effective diet drug. We know of no experiments on this.

10 percent was eliminated unchanged in the urine if the chewers did not use alkali. If they did, the proportion rose to 22 percent to 35 percent. Some researchers believe that when cocaine is absorbed through the digestive tract, as in coca chewing, it is partly broken down to ecgonine and benzoylecgonine even before it reaches the bloodstream and is carried to the brain. But this is still in doubt.[13]

5

THE ACUTE

INTOXICATION

IN RECOUNTING the history and pharmacology of cocaine, we have necessarily mentioned most of the effects it can produce. Before discussing these effects more systematically and in more detail, we must distinguish several topics or dimensions of analysis. One of these is physiological versus psychological: roughly, effects on the involuntary functions of the organism versus effects on mood, perceptions, voluntary action, and higher mental activity. It must be remembered that the physiological and the psychological are merely ends of a continuum: many effects, like rise or decline in sexual interest, changes in power of endurance, or tendency toward restlessness or calm, are not easily identified as one or the other. Another important dimension is acute versus chronic intoxication: the effect of a single dose, large or small, as opposed to the effect of long continued use. Still another is the distinction between smaller and larger doses or "moderate" and "excessive" use. We put these words in quotation marks because they tend to be vague, misleading, and emotionally fraught. For many people there is simply no such thing as moderation in the use of certain drugs, and cocaine is one of them. We will return to this question when we contribute our opinion on the question of when and how cocaine is harmful or beneficent. Meanwhile we speak of moderate and excessive use of cocaine, or small and large doses, in the same common-sense way that most people—not, of course, prohibitionists—speak of small and large amounts of alcohol or moderate and excessive drinking. There are two other relevant distinctions. One is coca versus cocaine; the other is the difference among various methods of administration: subcutaneous or intravenous injection; sniffing; oral ingestion by eating, drinking, or chewing; and, more rarely, rubbing into the gums, smoking, and topical application to the genitals.

The three main continua or modes of distinction, then, are physiological-psychological, acute-chronic, and small dose-large dose or moderate-excessive. We shall try to evaluate the effects of cocaine in all these categories, paying attention where necessary to the differences between coca and cocaine and among various routes of access to the body. A classification like this cannot determine how and how much the drug actually is or will be used. That depends on conditions of availability and other rather indeterminate psychological and social factors. Although this statement seems obvious, we introduce it here because what it emphasizes is so often ignored; for example, the effect of an overdose of very strong hashish or pure tetrahydrocannabinol (the main active principle of the hemp plant) is discussed as though it were the typical effect of marihuana. Since cannabis is not often used that way, the picture of the situation is distorted even when the description is technically accurate. To judge a drug in context, we need more than an enumeration, even an orderly enumeration, of all the effects it has ever produced or might possibly produce; we must have some idea of how much it is going to be used, how, and by whom. This question involves the important and obscure subject of dependence, with its mixture of pharmacological, psychological, and social issues.

Individual variability and a shortage of information make it difficult to specify the dose of cocaine that is likely to produce a given effect. An amount that is barely a stimulant for one person may cause a mild paranoid reaction in another; in surgery an amount that produced only local anesthesia in most people was fatal to a few. Statistical or quantitative studies on the frequency of different reactions at different doses in human beings are simply not available, and we have only more or less anecdotal material—clinical case histories, interviews, and literary descriptions—and a few small-scale experiments on animals and human beings. Fortunately, new work is in progress, and much more information should be available in a few years.

Acute Effects of Cocaine

The euphoria produced by cocaine probably resembles amphetamine euphoria more than the effect of any other drug. But it is more transient: a single moderate dose (the average in recreational use is about 20 mg) might work for a half hour to an hour, as opposed to several hours for dextroamphetamine. It also tends to be subtler or milder than amphetamine, at least when taken orally or sniffed. Often the user feels little the first few times and has to learn to appreciate it; this is rare with amphetamines. A man we interviewed said, "Of course when I first snorted some coke I didn't get off on it, like most people, I've noticed. . . . I figured, well, there's got to be something to this, everybody really likes it . . . and after trial and error I just sort of started to perceive the subtle areas." Another statement: "The first time it was nothin' at all, didn't get off. It's very subtle, in the small amounts." Ernst Joël and F. Fränkel in their book *Der Cocainismus* confirm this. Gutiérrez-Noriega and Zapata Ortiz say that it often takes a few weeks to become sensitive to the effects of the coca leaf; they believe this implies an increasing failure of the liver to metabolize cocaine.[1] But probably the sensitization is mostly a matter of learning to perceive the effects, a phenomenon well known in connection with cannabis, opiates, and alcohol. People apparently take longer to learn to "read" cocaine than amphetamines, but less time than they need for opiates or cannabis. Many do report strong effects the first time they use the drug, especially if they have the opportunity to repeat the dose at intervals for a couple of hours. It is also worth mentioning again that the unreliable quality of illicit cocaine magnifies the apparent variability of its effect and sometimes gives a delusive impression of mildness or subtlety.

Arno Offerman, in an early (1926) controlled experiment testing the CNS effects of cocaine and other local anesthetics, administered cocaine in subcutaneous injections of 40 mg to 100 mg to a number of normal subjects, mostly physicians, as well as victims of various forms of schizophrenia and brain disease. In normal subjects the more or less consistent result was increased talkativeness and confidence, fast pulse and pounding heart, reduction of fatigue, and restlessness. A phlegmatic psychiatrist felt "as though he had drunk strong coffee" and talked more freely. The effect lasted 50 minutes. Another psychiatrist began to pace up and down and talk incessantly without ending his sentences or listening for replies. For about an hour, beginning 15 minutes after the injection, this state alternated with one in which he sat still in a corner staring into space, grimacing and chomping on his cigar butt. Still another psychiatrist said he saw everything more clearly, "as through a magnifying glass," and felt both physically strong and happy in such a way that he did not know which phenomenon was the cause of the other. A woman doctor began to rock back and forth on her chair, made little chewing and tongue motions, felt pleasantly restless, talked fast and continuously, sometimes in unfinished sentences, felt coquettish and turned her eyes with enlarged pupils on the experimenter, wanted to dance, and regarded her own behavior as affected and slightly ridiculous. The effect lasted two hours. A male physician felt lightness and a sense of well-being, a heightened emotional state, as though he could cry for joy. Offerman himself felt animated as after drinking alcohol but without the same giddiness or numbness, strong, and talkative. After half an hour he was tired and apathetic. He had no desire to eat for ten hours afterward. Except in the case of the woman doctor, the subjective effects began ten or fifteen minutes after injection and lasted from a half hour to an hour. Injections of saline solution administered to the same subjects under the same circumstances had no effect, and injections of synthetic local anesthetics had very little effect.[2]

Reports from literary sources and interviews may be less sober and the descriptive terms not always consistent, but the general tendency is the same: "It gives me a hilarious, exhilarating feeling"; "It's something like drinking but does not make me feel fuzzy like whiskey"; " 'Rich' is the only word to describe how he felt"; "that familiar snow feeling . . . I began to want to talk. Cocaine produces . . . an illusion of supreme well-being and a soaring overconfidence in both physical and mental ability. . . . There was also that feeling of timelessness"; "that pale cocaine edge, pale like acetylene flame . . . that voluminous hollow rush inside, that slippage of control systems, that cocaine express"; "It's good to do any job with a good attitude, with a happy frame of mind, positive energy"; "It's nothing more than stand-up-and-move energy. It's nothing that stands out as anything more than a good deep breath will do you"; "One thing you do, you get a lot of energy. So naturally you're gonna be almost like a racehorse at the gate, quivering inside"; "Depending on my mood, different aspects will be accentuated. There's obviously the speed quality . . . the first experience is a burning of the nose; then there's a kind of rush that goes straight to your brain, sort of a giddiness, a mild elation. After the rush, not exactly a speed high, but a feeling of being able to concentrate . . . I'd find myself smoking a lot more, just living at a faster, more intense pace . . . talking is a tremendous amount of fun"; "If I do some coke, I want to draw, write a poem, talk to people—it makes me verbal—I want to work things out, go places and do things. . . . I feel

like a vegetable without it. With it, I'm more in touch with my feelings";
"It's the biggest sense-of-humor dampener I've ever seen. . . . If you sit
around and blow joints all night and everybody gets real tired or something, and somebody pulls out some cocaine, everyone starts to talk and
go again, but the smiles go away. It's an edge, cocaine."

Here are some more comments. "I've taken a couple of snorts of heroin,
and all I can say, heroin is like the opposite. Because when you do cocaine, everything's *not* okay. There's a whole lot to do, the house is a
mess all of a sudden." "If I had to describe it in physical terms it's like sit-
ting in a field in Switzerland full of flowers, fresh spring grass, and the
wind is blowing, and it's chilly but it's beautiful, a brisk day. Dynamite."
"It has a positive effect on communication. . . . You can sit and talk for
hours and hours, and feel a total rapport with the person you're talking
to." "I do better with something which is beautiful in a subtle and quiet-
ing way [marihuana], rather than something which is beautiful in a
racy and flashy way, like coke . . . and sometimes . . . you pay for it . . .
you feel too much energy or something, just generally feel a little bit nervous or anxious. . . . I still don't know if maybe there's something that's
not meant for this world about that product, you know, like just being so
spiritual and so pleasurable that it may not be real, and life isn't meant to
be lived in absolutes like that. . . . I would consider it in a category totally
by itself, different from hallucinogens, different from other things like
speed, because coke is much more integratable with your normal life. If
you take acid, like you're just *gone* for 15 hours, and that's the way it is,
an isolated experience. But this is *not* an isolated experience, it's an in-
tegrated experience." "Rapport, ease of communication . . . I started
wanting to talk again." "It's the main ego-inflating drug there is." "Under
cocaine I feel like a king. I make plans of great ingenuity. I can move
about for hours." "You wouldn't know it, but when I don't take coke I'm
rather bashful." "There never was any elixir so instant magic as cocaine.
To one the drug may bring liveliness, to another languor, to another cre-
ative force, to another tireless energy, to another lust. But each in his way
is happy." Freud described his own experience this way: "The psychic effect of cocainum muriaticum in doses of .05 to .10 gram consists of exhilaration and lasting euphoria, which does not differ in any way from the
normal euphoria of a healthy person. . . . One is simply normal, and soon
finds it difficult to believe that one is under the influence of any drug at
all." [3]

These remarks, the purple passages as well as the sober ones, are about
cocaine eaten, sniffed, or taken subcutaneously. Intravenous injection
produces even more immediate and striking effects. "An intoxicating

wave of the highest rapture . . . at this moment the world seems perfect." "The first time I ever did it, I shot it. . . . It's very remarkable, it doesn't last very long. It's a very intense rush, a very *very* intense rush. If you're standing up, you can conceivably fall over. Very very intense rush. It just sits you in your seat, for ten or fifteen minutes, blissed out." "Just started as a *zoom* up . . . after the zoom up, it was like a thing that we call, you hear bells, your ears started ringin' and you dealt with that for two or three minutes, and then . . . you level off, and then things was just bright . . . that strange, magical feeling . . . I used coke for that *zoom* and that strange feeling." William Burroughs describes it more artfully in *Naked Lunch*:

> Ever pop coke in the mainline? It hits you right in the brain, activating connections of pure pleasure. The pleasure of morphine is in the viscera. You listen down into yourself after a shot. But C is electricity through the brain, and the C yen is of the brain alone, a need without body and without feeling. The C-charged brain is a berserk pinball machine, flashing blue and pink lights in electric orgasm. C pleasure could be felt by a thinking machine, the first hideous stirrings of insect life.

And in an article on drugs for the *British Journal of Addiction* written in 1956 and later appended to the Grove Press edition of the novel, Burroughs wrote:

> Cocaine is the most exhilarating drug I have ever used. The euphoria centers in the head. Perhaps the drug activates pleasure connections directly in the brain. I suspect that an electric current in the right place would produce the same effect. The full exhilaration of cocaine can only be realized by an intravenous injection. The pleasurable effects do not last more than five or ten minutes. If the drug is injected into the skin, rapid elimination vitiates the effects. The same goes double for sniffing.[4]

Acute Effects of Coca

At the other end of the emotional and rhetorical scale, the solemn, taciturn, introverted people of the Peruvian and Bolivian highlands rarely admit that coca does anything except reduce hunger, thirst, and fatigue. There is in fact some doubt about how much cocaine is actually entering their digestive tracts and bloodstreams. According to the report of the United Nations Commission of 1950, the average daily consumption of coca leaf is 50 to 100 grams, with a few old *coqueros* chewing as much as 250 grams. A 1948 study found that in each *cocada* an average of 34 grams of leaves was chewed, with 180 mg of alkaloids including 112 mg of cocaine; the study concluded that coca chewers ingest 200 to 500 mg of cocaine daily. In a recent study of ten families of coca chewers in a town in southern Peru, Joel M. Hanna found the average consumption to be 60 grams of coca leaves, or 250 mg of cocaine, daily. The estimates of the total production of coca leaves and number of coca users given in Chapter 1 suggest an average of 30 to 80 grams a day; more coca illegally converted to cocaine would lower the mean, and a larger number of occasional or intermittent users would imply a higher mean consumption among those who take the drug daily. This is a substantial amount (the 250 mg of cocaine a day used by Hanna's subjects might cost $20 in the United States), and it is sometimes questioned why the apparent effect is not greater.[5]

One possibility suggested by experiments is that oral cocaine is not absorbed well. For example, in a 1971 study subcutaneous cocaine increased the motor activity of mice at 10 mg per kg, while oral cocaine did not affect it even at 50 mg per kg. The drug improved learning of a flight reaction when administered by either route. Parenteral and oral cocaine were equally effective in reducing fatigue as measured by reflex reaction time. Oral caffeine and amphetamines, in contrast with oral cocaine, do increase spontaneous motor activity in mice at relatively low doses. Recent experiments by Robert M. Post and his colleagues on depressed patients suggest that cocaine taken orally up to 200 mg a day produces no consistent mood change, although it modifies sleep patterns. These experiments were controlled and double-blind, but the subjects were of course not normal. Freud experienced some euphoria when he drank 50 to 100 mg in a water solution. The apparent relief of neurasthenia and other disturbances by coca wine or coca tea also implies that oral cocaine is effective. Gutiérrez-Noriega and Zapata Ortiz believe that cocaine is absorbed well by the digestive system and even contend that the difference between the lethal oral dose and the lethal subcutaneous dose in dogs is *less* than it is for other drugs of the same type: a ratio of 2:1 or 1.5:1. One and a half mg per kg of oral cocaine (110 mg in a 150-pound man), they state, usually produce some euphoria and faster reaction times in human beings. More thorough experimental studies are needed to determine whether and in what respects the effect of cocaine is different or weaker when it is taken by mouth.[6]

A question that arises in this connection is the function of the *llipta* or *tocra*—the alkaline substance used in chewing coca. It may be activating oral cocaine that would otherwise be ineffective. Analysis of its chemical composition shows that potassium and calcium compounds are the effective agents.[7] Two main explanations for the use of alkali have been proposed: 1) it helps to extract the alkaloids from the organic acids that bind them in the leaf; 2) it facilitates absorption of the extracted alkaloids into the bloodstream from the digestive tract. The second seems more plausible on the available evidence. In one experiment, 14 men chewed 20 grams of leaves each; eight used alkali (bicarbonate of soda) and six did not. The subjects who did not use alkali eliminated an average of 11.8 mg of cocaine in the urine in the first six hours after they began to chew; the others eliminated an average of 19.8 mg. The amount of alkaloids (mostly cocaine) extracted from the leaf, as measured by chemical analysis of samples before and after chewing, was about the same in both groups. Without alkali, subjects eliminated in the urine 10 to 20 percent of the cocaine they ingested; with alkali, urinary elimination of unchanged cocaine reached 22 to 35 percent. The experimenters concluded that the alkali speeds the absorption of cocaine into the bloodstream and therefore its elimination.[8]

Emilio Ciuffardi made the most thorough study of the effect of alkaline substances. He had 124 *coqueros* chew their accustomed amount, 71 of them with *tocra* (*quinoa* ashes) and 53 without it. (He notes that those who were not given *tocra* protested and asked permission to use the *tocra* they had brought along). The proportion of alkaloids by weight in the leaves varied from 0.5 percent to 0.7 percent, of which about 80 percent was cocaine. The subjects who did not have *tocra* chewed for an average of 95 minutes; those who had it chewed for an average of 113 minutes. The average total of alkaloids ingested with *tocra* was 213 mg; the average without *tocra* was 272 mg. With *tocra* 87 percent of the alkaloids in the leaves chewed were extracted (ingested) and without *tocra* 83 percent. The smaller total amount of cocaine ingested with *tocra* had considerably more effect on pulse rate, body temperature, muscular vigor, and mood than the larger amount ingested without the alkali. Obviously the main function of the alkali was not to extract cocaine from the leaf but to facilitate absorption into the bloodstream, since the coca chewers who did not use *tocra* actually ingested more cocaine and other alkaloids in a shorter time but still failed to obtain the accustomed effect. In other experiments it appears that the lethal dose of cocaine is lower in an alkaline solution and higher in an acid one. *Tocra* apparently somehow prevents cocaine from being neutralized or destroyed in the stomach before it is absorbed into the blood.[9]

A related problem is the contribution of the associate alkaloids to the effect of coca. This is a matter of great interest to admirers of the drug like Mortimer and Richard T. Martin, who believe that the coca alkaloids work synergistically or that ecgonine, benzoylecgonine, and hygrines act directly on muscle tissues rather than through the central nervous system like cocaine.[10] Gutiérrez-Noriega, on the other hand, contends that coca has basically the same effect as cocaine. Freud agrees; a large dose of ecgonine, incidentally, had little effect on him.[11] Ecgonine has the same legal status as cocaine, but that is presumably because cocaine is easily synthesized from it. There is no experimental evidence on the volatile aromatic hygrine alkaloids that Mortimer considers so important, but one study is available comparing the effects of ecgonine, benzoylecgonine, and cocaine in mice. The lethal dose of ecgonine proves to be very high, about 4 grams per kg intravenously; 1 gram per kg has no apparent effect at all. (These doses are the equivalent of 280 grams and 70 grams respectively in a 150-pound man). On a test of the grasping reflex used to measure fatigue and a test of conditioned learning, ecgonine at suitably high doses improved performance, although to a lesser degree than cocaine. Benzoylecgonine, which is chemically intermediate between cocaine and ecgonine, is also intermediate in its effect on learning and fatigue.[12]

The most interesting result of this experiment was that cocaine administered orally at low doses had effects like those of ecgonine; it was concluded that digestive juices turn most of the cocaine into benzoylecgonine and ecgonine before it is absorbed.[13] The function of *llipta* or *tocra*, then, may be to create an alkaline solution that permits absorption of the cocaine into the bloodstream before it is partly broken down into the relatively inactive benzoylecgonine and ecgonine.

But there is little evidence that the associate alkaloids in the coca leaf itself either moderate the effect of cocaine considerably or produce substantial effects of their own. It has not been shown that any common use of the coca leaf cannot be duplicated by cocaine in suitable doses and methods of administration; therefore there may not be any phenomena that need to be explained by the synergistic action of several alkaloids. Cocaine is not only the most active alkaloid but the one present in by far the greatest amount; it constitutes about 80 percent of the alkaloid content. As for the possible moderating effects of this relatively small proportion of other alkaloids, none have been found. A purified alkaloid mixture from the leaf was administered subcutaneously to 42 rats in a dose of 300 mg per kg, the amount of cocaine hydrochloride previously determined to be lethal 50 percent of the time in that form. The effects were qualitatively the same as those of pure cocaine hydrochloride, and 40.4 percent of the rats died.[14] Further research would be useful, but we must con-

clude for now that the associate alkaloids in the leaf do not have an important pharmacological role.

The defenders of coca are correct in stating that it rarely produces the
more lurid symptoms of acute or chronic cocaine abuse. The obvious
reason is that it is impossible to absorb enough cocaine into the bloodstream fast enough that way. Pure chemicals taken by injection, sniffing,
or smoking have more immediate, powerful, and dangerous effects than
plant matter containing only small quantities of these chemicals and entering the bloodstream by the normal digestive route for the absorption of
alien substances. (The defenses of the gastrointestinal tract against cocaine, as we saw, seem to create the need for alkali in chewing coca.) Eating opium does not give even the same effect as smoking it, much less
the sudden, strong euphoria of a morphine injection; most people drink
coffee, beer, and wine, but no one injects caffeine or ethyl alcohol into his
arm. These distinctions may have something to do with the modifying effects of subsidiary alkaloids and other plant substances. Andrew Weil observes:

> There is no question that if the only form of sugar available to us were the
> whole raw kind, our total sugar intake would be a fraction of what it is now.
> The immediate sensory signals coming from the secondary compounds of the
> whole plant tell you not to overdo it. They provide a kind of insulation from the
> highly reinforcing properties of sucrose. I suspect that the secondary alkaloids
> in opium likewise help people not to overdo the use of morphine, and I feel sure
> that the many coca alkaloids play a similar role with respect to cocaine.[15]

But this remains speculative; the distinct effects are more obviously explained by differences in the concentration of the active compound and
the speed of its absorption. Probably the social context of the use of a drug
in one form rather than another and the fears and expectations surrounding it (for example, attitude toward hypodermic needles) are also important. The relation between these factors and the concentration and route
of absorption is, of course, a sociological and historical problem, not a
pharmacological one.

The reticence of Peruvian and Bolivian Indians about the effect of coca
on their mood cannot be regarded as evidence that it has no effect. Even
the early Spanish chroniclers noticed the difference between their reserved, solemn character and the ebullience and (at first) friendliness of
the coastal natives. This passivity, or shyness, or dignity, or apathy, or
melancholy, or aloofness—how one decides to describe it probably depends on cultural bias—is heightened by the natural suspicion among
oppressed people about the intentions of outsiders who come to inves-

tigate their habits. Gutiérrez-Noriega, who made the most extensive studies of the effects of coca on its habitual users, confesses that they almost uniformly deny any psychological effects at first, so that it is difficult to get information from them. But he persisted and, with the help of auxiliary experimental studies and investigations carried out among inhabitants of the coastal areas, obtained testimony to some of the same effects that cocaine users describe.

In one study Gutiérrez-Noriega examined 30 men, all poor peasants. One-third of them used 70 to 120 grams of coca leaf a day, and two-thirds used 30 to 70 grams. They all said it suppressed hunger, thirst, and fatigue. Many said it made them feel stronger and took away their worries: "With coca I forget my troubles, while with liquor it's the opposite." It tended to intensify the association of ideas, and it produced optimism and confidence. A few reported changes in the visual field—mostly, objects seemed to stand out in relief and space became larger. Time sometimes seemed to be speeded up. The effect lasted one to two hours and was often followed by fatigue.[16]

Gutiérrez-Noriega also made a study of 25 men in Lima, 20 of them prisoners in the local jails, who used coca at the rate of 50 to 100 grams a day. The difference in temperaments and social setting obviously mattered a great deal. The prisoners produced descriptions that resemble Mantegazza's in some ways more closely than they resemble the Andean peasants'. They often found colors brighter and had a sense of proximity to the faraway. There might be a sense of a presence without visual content; for example, a feeling that an enemy was at one's side. Many of them reported fantastic visions or hallucinations, which they never confused with actual perceptions. One described his visions as "beautiful landscapes and golden castles." Street noises might turn into voices or melody or the steps of a pursuing policeman. The body seemed bigger, stronger, more agile—some used the word *superhombre* ("superman"). The slang term these men used for the intoxicated state, incidentally, is *armado,* which means literally "armed" but might be translated "loaded" or "charged up." The corresponding term in the United States is "high" or, at a more advanced stage of intoxication, "wired" or "cranked up." Coca produced quick but uncontrolled association of ideas and illusions of superior intelligence. It also sometimes induced fantasies of wealth or sexual fantasies. But one *coquero* is also quoted as saying, "Coca increases self-control, alcohol makes you lose it."[17]

Some skepticism about these reports is necessary. Gutiérrez-Noriega tended to exaggerate the effects of coca, which he wanted to abolish; the Lima criminals were probably not the most reliable of men and may have been telling him what they thought he wanted to hear. Unfortunately, he does not specify dosages after he has mentioned the average (moderate) consumption of 50 to 100 grams a day. Some of his descriptions sound like the effects not of a few grams of coca leaf but of a fairly large dose of pure cocaine working on highly impressionable personalities. Not even the heaviest cocaine users we interviewed reported anything like fantastic visions. Still, the possibility that they might occur is confirmed by Mantegazza's testimony and by comments like this one from the nineteenth-century traveler Poeppig about his *mestizo* guide: "His description of the beautiful images that came to him at night in the woods and the depiction of his glorious feelings at such times had something truly terrifying about them." [18]

In another study of coca users, Francisco Risemberg Mendizábal describes the coca effect much more soberly. He finds a period of extraversion and euphoria at the start of chewing followed by a desire to be alone and withdrawal into oneself because of the multitude of thoughts passing through the mind. The *coqueros* only appear to be gloomy, he writes; their imagination is soaring. They can work without boredom for hours at a mechanical task because, in the words of one of them, they "are not there." When Risemberg Mendizábal asked coca users what they would most like to do when in that state, many of them answered: drink alcohol. None of the men he interviewed had experienced any symptoms of intoxication from excess chewing. [19]

For a firsthand report from a coca chewer who is not a South American Indian, here is an account provided to us by Andrew Weil:

> Next to my typewriter is a bag of dry coca leaves sent to me by a friend who purchased them in the marketplace of Huanuco, a town in Central Peru. I take a small handful of them and place them in my mouth, moistening them and working them into a wad. Over the next few minutes I add more leaves until I have a walnut-sized mass. Now I add a small chunk of grayish-black material also from the Huanuco market. It is called *tocra* and consists of the ashes of the stalks of a cereal plant cultivated in the Andes. The salty taste of tocra blends well with the distinctive flavor of coca, and its alkalinity will increase the effects of the leaves.
>
> I keep my quid of coca between cheek and teeth, working it from time to time to suck the juices from it. I do not swallow the leaves. I savor the taste for I have good associations to it. Within a few minutes a pleasant tingling and numbness permeate the inside of my mouth and spread down my throat, a sign that the leaves are releasing their activity. In another few minutes I am aware of a delicious feeling in my stomach, a sort of warm contentment not wholly unlike the sensation that persists in my mouth. Now I feel a subtle energy moving from my stomach through my muscles. My mind is clear and alert. My mood picks up. I turn my attention to my typewriter and enthusiastically begin

to write. In half an hour or so I will have sucked my quid of leaves dry of their virtues. Then I will spit them out and rinse my mouth. The subtle stimulation I now feel will continue for perhaps an hour, then will fade gradually and imperceptibly without leaving me different from normal. My mouth will feel clean and refreshed. I will not chew coca again until I wish to use its stimulation for some other specific purpose.[20]

Summary of the Cocaine Feeling

Gutiérrez-Noriega is probably exaggerating when he declares that coca produces an "illusory satisfaction of desires . . . giving an impression of vivid reality so perfect that it provides genuine relief in the most adverse circumstances of life." It is easier to agree when he writes, "The drug does not . . . display any predetermined tendency to develop any particular type of feeling. The latter depends . . . on the content and quality of the thoughts and fantasies through which the subject passes. . . . It also depends on the company in which he finds himself and other social factors." In this respect moderate doses of cocaine are no different from moderate doses of opium, alcohol, or other psychoactive drugs. One person may become garrulous, another contemplative. One may feel rapture, another nervousness. One may want to sit still, another to pace or dance. Offerman in fact described the effect of cocaine as "an almost comically heightened amplification of one's character and individual predispositions," as though the drug turned a man into a caricature of himself.[21]

But in spite of all ambiguity and variability, the cocaine feeling cannot be confused in the long run with the physical relaxation and emotional disinhibition induced by alcohol or the placid, drowsy opiate sensation, or even the relatively long-lasting and physically intense excitement produced by amphetamines. It is characterized most by heightened self-confidence and a feeling of mastery. One writer put it this way: "With cocaine, one is indeed master of everything, but everything matters intensely. With heroin, the feeling of mastery increases to such a point that nothing matters at all." [22] Another way to put it is that opiates tend to cause a loss of interest in the self that makes mastery of the external environment irrelevant: the feeling is a kind of Nirvana. In contrast, a stimulant like cocaine heightens the sensory and emotional brightness and distinctness of the self against its environmental ground. A man we interviewed described it this way: "I knew that everyone knew *I* was

there; I thought that everyone could *see* me. Everything became alive."
This strong focal awareness may degenerate into paranoia with delusions
of reference: everything and everybody seem to be threatening "me," the
object of greatest interest in the universe. The heightening of the sense
of self—"the greatest ego-inflating drug there is"—may be a correlate in
the mind of the sympathomimetic action of stimulants. For in moments
of stress and danger the organism has to concentrate its forces to pre-
serve itself against a suddenly hostile environment. It must *realize* its
own distinctness from the world and discourage any tendency toward a
relaxed merging with it. In the mind this may produce a strong sense of
individuality and of power and control, and a drug that simulates the central as well as the peripheral effects of sympathetic arousal will do the
same.

This phenomenon may be accompanied by joy, anger, even anxiety or
fear, or a mixture of all these: "It [cocaine] makes my mind ten times
quicker than normal, but also makes me anxious"; "It makes me jumpy
and scary, but I like it." [23] In a famous experiment, the effect of injections
of epinephrine on a group of subjects proved to be dependent on the behavior of a confederate of the experimenter who was in the room with
them. If he seemed happy, they felt happy; if he acted angry or annoyed,
they became ill-tempered too. In a control group that received placebos,
there was no such contagion of emotions.[24] The moral about the importance of the social component in the experience induced by psychoactive
drugs is obvious. But the experiment also shows that even the definition
of a physiological phenomenon, especially one that mimics the effect of
stress, as this or that emotion depends on personality and setting. The
coward defines the coursing of epinephrine and norepinephrine through
his body as fear, and the brave man defines it as the joy of battle or the exhilaration of facing danger. The fighter pilot, the racing driver, and the
mountain climber are often seeking the kind of exhilaration, the sense of
living more intensely, that comes from putting one's life in danger. Central stimulant drugs are less equivocal in their effects than injected epinephrine (which does not easily cross the physiological barrier between
the bloodstream and the brain) or stress, because they apparently influence the arousal and pleasure centers of the brain before they affect rage
and fear mechanisms. But the exhilaration they produce has the same
source as the pleasures of adventure (not, of course, that people think
they are risking their lives when they use cocaine). This effect, combined
with the further adventure of performing an illicit act, may contribute to
the interest in cocaine, especially among adolescents. The various emotions, or rather interpretations, associated with catecholamines (and

therefore with drugs that affect them) may also coexist in the same person at successive moments or even at the same moment. André Gide once wrote, "The hare or deer pursued by another animal takes pleasure in its running, its leaps, and its feints." This beautifully expresses the emotional ambiguity of sympathetic nervous system activity by referring it to the condition of creatures that have no words for joy or fear.

Effects on Intellectual and Physical Performance

Like other stimulants, cocaine gives a feeling of improved intellectual and physical capacity that is often of doubtful validity. It "makes you feel superior to other people," as one man we interviewed said. Another reported:

> It's efficient, it's an effector. On all levels. A potentiator. . . . If I'm going to do a large amount of coke, then I should be in a position in which I am actively communicating, or receiving. . . . Like if you're going to get into writing, or performing, or something like that . . . it's a level on which you become much more fluid, you have a whole lot more psychic poise and mental agility and physical agility. . . . It's not something that you don't know what's happening. You *do* know what's happening . . . and you're in control. . . . Cocaine gives me a feeling of mental, psychic comprehension, a level of confidence, of competence, a unity of my own work, my own validity.

On the other hand, a male cocaine user commented about attracting women, "You snort so you can pull your rap on her. My rap wasn't any better on cocaine, but see, I thought it was." Malcolm X, in his *Autobiography*, recounts how a foolish overconfidence induced by cocaine caused him to walk up to his white mistress in a public place and talk to her while she was with a friend of her husband's. He thinks the husband would have killed him if he had not been arrested the same day. And William Burroughs, who has certain artistic and intellectual achievements to his credit as well as a broad acquaintance with psychoactive drugs, considers the strong CNS stimulants useless for serious work: "Amphetamines and cocaine are quite worthless for writing and nothing of value remains." [25]

Almost all the evidence about cocaine's effect on performance is anecdotal; but it seems to be qualitatively similar to that of other stimulants like amphetamines and caffeine, which have been studied in controlled experiments and are relatively well understood. The experiments show that both drugs, and especially amphetamines, often improve performance on fairly simple intellectual and physical tasks. They do not enhance the quality of more complicated intellectual work (although they may speed it up) and may even lower it by inducing anxiety, restlessness, or overestimation of one's capacities. Amphetamines in particular can increase the endurance of athletes and enhance their performance in the short run, at the possible cost of eventually overstraining their physical capacities. Amphetamines reduce reaction time, hasten conditioned learning, and increase the rate of learning a motor skill. They also improve arithmetic calculation. But they have no effect on general intellectual capacity as measured by IQ and other intelligence tests.[26]

What little is known about cocaine in this area confirms the expected resemblances. It improves attention, reaction time, and speed in certain simple intellectual performances. For example, Johannes Lange in 1920 found that as little as 20 mg by mouth reduced the time taken on an arithmetic calculating test and on a word-association test produced more associations (but also more superficial ones—for example, sound rather than meaning). Hans W. Maier, also working in the 1920s, tested a habitual cocaine user on addition problems after giving her 400 mg at one time and 650 mg at another time (apparently by mouth). Cocaine greatly increased the number of additions completed, from 33.5 per minute without the drug, to 42.2 per minute with 400 mg, to 57.4 per minute with 650 mg. It also doubled the number of mistakes, from four to eight out of a total of about 700; this suggests that cocaine, like amphetamines, can give speed at the expense of accuracy. In two other experiments, also on habitual cocaine users, cocaine (20 mg sniffed) produced better scores than no drug or cocoa, but worse than coffee or even nearly caffeine-free coffee. Maier concluded that the nervousness caused by cocaine sometimes impaired performance, but he believed that it directly excited associative activity in the mind.[27] Twenty years later Vicente Zapata Ortiz studied sensory reaction time and attention under the influence of oral cocaine in 13 coca chewers and 13 controls. Sensory reaction time slowed in both groups but on a test of attention both groups worked faster and the coca chewers also made fewer errors than they had made without the drug. Zapata Ortiz suggests that the divergence between the two tests may be caused by a tendency to distraction by fantasizing that worked more strongly on the former. Incidentally, coca chewers were slow on both tests compared to nonusers, even under the influence of cocaine.[28]

For mental work that requires wakefulness, a free flow of associations, or the suppression of boredom and fatigue, a drug like cocaine is undoubtedly useful. The secretary who drinks several cups of coffee a day at the office in order not to fall asleep over the typewriter, Balzac sustaining himself on caffeine for the production of novel after novel, and John Kennedy enhancing his "vigor" with amphetamines were making use of this property of stimulants. In the late nineteenth and early twentieth centuries a number of writers and intellectuals obviously used cocaine in this way. If Freud wrote his cocaine papers, General Grant his *Memoirs,* or old Leo XIII his papal encyclicals under the influence of cocaine, it was serving the same function for them that coffee served for Balzac and many others. Freud wrote that cocaine "steels one to intellectual effort." [29] It was for this reason that students sometimes used cocaine, as they now use amphetamines, to get through examinations. An interview subject told us:

> SUBJECT: I wrote a whole entire master's thesis, a hundred pages on Samuel Beckett, and got an honorable mention on the thing. And I wrote it in seven days, start to finish, with about a gram of coke. . . . And I never could have written it otherwise, because I couldn't understand how all these various ideas fit together. . . . I never wrote so fast in my life. . . . I didn't eat and I didn't sleep. I like broke the thing up into three parts, maybe two days each, and after two days of just constant work, I would like take a Valium, and just sleep till I woke up. . . .
>
> INTERVIEWER: It aided your creativity?
>
> SUBJECT: Maybe it reduced it, maybe it reduced all the thoughts in my head to a clear line of action, which gave me a theme, which I didn't have before. . . .

But no drug will provide intellectual capacity, talent, or genius where it is lacking; that is where the illusory aspect of the mental stimulant effect becomes obvious. Euphoria and confidence can make the user attribute to the drug effects that have nothing to do with it and cause him to overestimate the value of the changes it does produce. Conan Doyle seems to have been conscious of this when he had Sherlock Holmes say, after calling cocaine "transcendentally stimulating and clarifying to the mind," that he never used the drug when he was working on a case. William Burroughs, as we noted, has also testified against the use of cocaine and amphetamines for intellectual work. The delusive overestimation of one's capacities that stimulants can produce has been amply documented in the case of amphetamines.[30] After chronic stimulant abuse, as William Halsted's own later estimate of his condition when he was taking large doses of cocaine shows, intellectual faculties may be directly disrupted. In Chapter 2 we quoted the first sentence of one of his papers written at that time. It suggests a man in a mentally disjointed, confused, distracted state. When we discuss chronic abuse of cocaine more fully in Chapter 6, we will provide other examples of this effect.

Cocaine may improve performance in several kinds of tasks that contain elements of both the mental and the physical. One of these is routine, unvarying, repetitious labor that nevertheless requires mental concentration. A man we interviewed said, "I know people who have shot coke and cleaned their whole house, you know. They get that up feeling, and then they start emptyin' ashtrays. Next thing you know they's cleaning the tables, next thing you know they's washing windows. . . . I've gotten into that, when it's good coke." It is possible, as we have mentioned, to induce incessant stereotyped turning, gnawing, or sniffing in rats, cats, and dogs by means of amphetamines or cocaine. The fact that amphetamines in large doses can sometimes cause absorption in routine activities that seem meaningless to the outsider is so notorious that a Swedish psychiatrist has suggested a special name for the phenomenon: "punding." Animal experiments indicate that cocaine produces less of this stereotyped behavior than amphetamines, but some remarks made in our interviews suggest at least a mild form of it. We shall discuss this further in another context.

A strong CNS stimulant can also fortify body and soul, at least in the short run, for the kind of performance in which boldness, confidence, and a feeling of mastery are themselves a large part of the achievement. A stimulant may eliminate the stage fright of the actor or musician, the timidity that suppresses the potential eloquence of a public speaker, the hesitancy that keeps the salesman from making his sale or the criminal from going through with his crime. Cocaine, like amphetamines, is often found useful when a performance in the colloquial sense—a good showing or a good show—is needed. This has been one of the greatest merits or temptations of the drug for its users ever since the days of advertisements recommending it "for young persons afflicted with timidity in society." A former actor told us, "You have at your command more of yourself. Say you're an actor, and you're going over a speech, and you've worked on it, and then you take a blow, and you go through the same speech. You will do it better." Another interview subject said, "To realize your own powers depends 90 percent on confidence. . . . When I ski, I don't consider confidence or energy derived from use of cocaine as misleading. Because the confidence that I need to get through a slalom course . . . the more aggressive I am, the better I ski. And the less hassle I have—I'm not going any faster. . . . It's just that my attitude is aggressive." No one recognizes the virtues of a performance in this sense better than actors and musicians, and from Adelina Patti and Sarah Bernhardt to the rock singers and Hollywood stars of today they have been prominent among the users of CNS stimulants. So have the producers, directors, talent agents, writers, and other auxiliary personnel of what is called show business. As we have mentioned, cocaine is now the stimulant they prize most, for reasons of fashion as well as its intrinsic psychopharmacological properties.

Effects like these are hard to define and almost impossible to test; the fact that cocaine eliminates fatigue and permits the user to continue physical activity more intensely or for a longer time is more obvious and universally recognized. Freud wrote:

> The main use of coca will undoubtedly remain that which the Indians have made of it for centuries: it is of value in all cases where the primary aim is to increase the physical capacity of the body for a given short period of time and to hold strength in reserve to meet further demands—especially when outward circumstances exclude the possibility of obtaining the rest and nourishment normally necessary for great exertion. . . . . Coca is a far more potent and far less harmful stimulant than alcohol.[31]

Freud did not distinguish between coca and cocaine. Today cocaine is rarely used merely to stay awake or increase physical capacity; for those who are willing to chance the dangers of strong drugs for this purpose, amphetamines are more effective and certainly cheaper. Only if staying awake implies going directly from work to an all-night party, or increasing physical capacity suggests permitting the user to dance for hours, can it be said that cocaine is commonly used in this way. For example, although professional athletes undoubtedly use the drug during off hours, we have seen no reports of their sniffing it before games. The nineteenth-century example of the Toronto Lacrosse Club and the French bicyclists sipping "Velo-Coca" is not (or not yet) being followed today, although a man wearing a T-shirt with the legend "Enjoy Cocaine" was recently seen running in the Boston Marathon.

But, as Freud indicates, for centuries cocaine (in the form of coca) was recognized mainly as a physical stimulant. Before the invention of the amphetamines, it was possibly the most potent stimulant drug available. We have mentioned a number of references to the physical capacities of men under the influence of coca. J. J. von Tschudi, the archaeologist who visted Peru in 1838–1842 and left us some of the most substantial information on coca chewing from the nineteenth century, mentioned a 62-year-old *coquero* who worked on diggings with him for five days and nights with only two hours of sleep a night and no food, ran tirelessly alongside a briskly stepping mule for 23 leagues (stopping only to chew coca), and then announced that he would do more of the same work if Tschudi would give him more coca.[32] We have also mentioned the experiment undertaken by the 78-year-old Sir Robert Christison in 1876 and reported in the *British Medical Journal* and later by Freud. Christison tired himself to the point of exhaustion by walking 15 miles without food. When he took the same walk after chewing coca, he arrived home after nine hours without food or drink neither tired nor suffering from thirst and hunger. He woke the next morning refreshed. Further testimony comes from a Bolivian writing in the United Nations *Bulletin on Narcotics*, a publication not ordinarily favorable to the coca leaf: "During the Chaco War [1929–1932], coca chewing among the *mestizo* and white Bolivian soldiers was widespread. I have experienced its beneficial effects myself on forced marches." Even Gutiérrez-Noriega, who was hostile toward the coca habit, concluded after self-experimentation that the drug could relieve fatigue temporarily without any serious depression afterward.[33]

Freud was one of the first to test quantitatively the effect of cocaine on physical capacity. He used a dynamometer, a machine that measures the motor power of the arm, and served as his own experimental subject. Fifty to 100 mg of cocaine hydrochloride (apparently taken by mouth, although he does not say) produced a considerable increase in motor power that began 15 minutes after the drug was taken and lasted in diminishing degree for some hours. Cocaine also shortened the time it took him to react by a hand motion to a sound signal. A few other experiments have confirmed the anecdotal evidence and Freud's work. Gutiérrez-Noriega found that resistance to fatigue in dogs, as measured by the length of time they would keep swimming in order to avoid drowning, was increased from 69 percent to 150 percent by cocaine at 4 mg per kg subcutaneously (the equivalent of 280 mg in a 150-pound man), a result similar to the effect of caffeine at 8 mg per kg. Testing athletes with a bicycle ergometer, Dore Thiel and Bertha Essig found that cocaine increased endurance. Robert Herbst and Paul Schellenberg found that cocaine speeded recuperation after hard labor.[34] More carefully controlled experiments are needed, especially comparisons of cocaine and amphetamines in various doses and methods of administration. The little evidence that is available, including most notably the reports of people who have taken both drugs, suggests that amphetamines have stronger physical effects.

The question of whether stimulants improve performance directly or by indirect action that primarily affects confidence and interest has proved obscure. For example, Freud noted that although his strength under the influence of cocaine might exceed the maximum it could attain under normal conditions, the increase was greatest when his general conditon was poor. He concluded that the action of the drug was not "a direct one—possibly on the motor nerve substance or on the muscles— but indirect, effected by an improvement of the general state of well-being." But C. Jacobi, writing in 1931, observed that doses of coca or cocaine too small to produce perceptible central stimulation nevertheless made work easier; he concluded that the effect was related to the periph- eral nerves and not to the brain. Joel M. Hanna, in a recent experiment using a bicycle ergometer, found no significant endurance differences between men who were chewing coca and men who were not, except that the coca chewers performed slightly longer at the very highest level of effort. He concluded that coca does not actually improve work perfor- mance but only reduces fatigue sensations and makes labor seem less burdensome.[35] Amphetamines work particularly well on experimental subjects who are bored, which suggests a primary effect on mood; but they also improve performance in an athletic competition like the shot put, where neither boredom nor physical fatigue in the ordinary sense is likely to be decisive; yet there is no evidence that they have any signifi- cant direct effect on skeletal muscles.

One way of resolving these issues is to refer to the connection between stimulant drug effects and those of an emergency situation. In moments of danger or stress people sometimes perform feats otherwise beyond their physical and mental capacity—whether or not they claim afterward to have felt unusual euphoria or confidence. It would be absurd to ask someone whether the catecholamines released in his body and brain made him "more favorably disposed" toward, say, saving his life in a moment of mortal danger, as though it were a matter for decision. In this case the attitude and the action are simply two aspects of the same pro- cess, a psychological-physiological unity. The verbal elaborations pro- duced by the cerebral cortex that are usually used in experiments as evi- dence of attitude or disposition are related to the attitude expressed *in* the action performed only in a complex and indirect fashion. There is no dis- tinct performance-improving effect separable from attitude in every sense; one cannot do something unusual without in some sense feeling different. On the other hand, euphoria, interest, or confidence as indi- cated by words or thoughts need have no *causal* relationship with im- provement in performances that are mostly the work of nonlinguistic and often noncortical brain areas. Short-term increases in physical and men- tal capacity under the influence of cocaine probably resemble the similar increases that sometimes occur under the influence of stress and danger;

they are neither more nor less genuine, they are achieved neither more nor less directly, and they have the same limitations.

The long-term effects of cocaine on endurance and work performance are less clear. However, it is known that stimulants cannot save energy but only redistribute its expenditure. Eventually the body has to "come down" at best or "crash" at worst. It is possible to regulate one's intake of the drug judiciously so that one works harder or feels more vigorous while taking it and sleeps a little longer or feels slightly tired when one is not. But it is impossible to avoid resting one's body for a long time, with or without stimulants, and not pay the price in physical exhaustion. This is well documented in the case of amphetamine abuse, where the crash is often associated with extreme fatigue. Cocaine is apparently milder, but fatigue after excessive use is common enough. For example, "Jimmy," the cocaine dealer portrayed by Richard A. Woodley, preferred to come down while sleeping but was willing to tolerate a little depression. But toward the end of his association with Woodley, he was telling the writer that he was run down, tired, worn out. A doctor finally insisted that he get some rest, because he was exhausted from insomnia brought on by cocaine.[36]

Studies of the effects of habitual use of coca on the work performance of South American Indians, like all attempts to elucidate the unspectacular long-range consequences of a common practice, are plagued by the difficulty of isolating relevant variables. For example, if the men who use coca are also undernourished and underpaid, or alcoholics, they may work poorly even though the coca does them no harm. Opinion on the question in Peru and Bolivia varies greatly. The armies of these countries have forbidden coca to the troops (it was part of their rations until the 1930s), and the officers believe that this makes them stronger because they eat better. One wonders whether they eat better because they are not using coca or rather simply because for the first time in their lives they have enough food. The UN Commission report quotes a Peruvian Director of Mines as saying that coca chewers are not employed in the mines at any but the simplest tasks, and it reports that the president of the Agricultural Society at Cuzco believes men who do not chew to be more efficient and intelligent. Some mine foremen consider *coqueros* to be dull, inattentive, accident-prone workmen. But many priests, physicians, and other professional men consider coca harmless.[37] In general the quality and quanitity of labor produced by *coqueros* is not impressive (according to Gutiérrez-Noriega, the average working day is only five hours), but there are so many plausible reasons for this—we will discuss them in another context—that it seems dubious to single out the coca leaf.

Besides relieving fatigue, cocaine "satisfies the hungry": that is, it tends to make hunger easier to bear and also to deaden appetite, partly by anesthetizing the palate and tongue but mainly by acting on the hypothalamic hunger center. A man we interviewed said, "You don't eat, you don't sleep enough. . . . I was down to like a hundred pounds. People were really freaked by it." Richard Schultes of Harvard University, an authority on psychoactive plant substances who chewed the coca leaf on and off for eight years while he was in South America in the 1940s, recounted to us two incidents in which his canoe tipped over in rapids and all his food was lost. In one case he had coca to chew, and four days of paddling without food but with coca was much less of an ordeal than three days of paddling without food or coca—more, he believes, because he felt less hunger than because he felt less fatigue. People in the coca-chewing regions of the Andes do not eat much, and there has been acrimonious controversy about whether their low calorie intake is a cause or a consequence of the coca, or neither, or both, and in any case how harmful it is. We will discuss this in Chapter 6. The appetite-deadening effect is another area where experiment is badly needed. It would be particularly interesting if tolerance to it proved to develop less quickly than tolerance to the anorectic action of amphetamines.

Sexual Effects

Sexuality is notoriously a playground of legend and rumor, because interest is nearly universal and the amount of reliable information most people have about other people's sexual activity never seems to be enough. The relationship between sex and psychoactive drugs is particularly obscure because the central nervous system is connected with sexual functions in such a complex and indirect way. Nowhere is the great individual variability in drug effects greater, and nowhere is the influence of temperament, culture, social circumstances, and, above all, expectations more important; this is familiar in the case of alcohol but less recognized for other drugs. Animal experiments are usually inadequate testing devices; for example, cannabis is anaphrodisiac in animals but many human users of the drug consider it aphrodisiac. The situation is further complicated and obscured when the use of a substance is illegal, as in the case of cocaine. Illegality invests a drug with the glamour of sinfulness, and insofar as sex is still regarded as sinful both the opponents of the drug and its users may associate it with what they may call excessive or better sex, depending on whether they approve of the sexual activity or the drug or the law. No doubt there are many people who wrongly believe that heroin is an aphrodisiac simply because they have been taught that it is an illicit pleasure that is dangerous, evil, and enjoyed by blacks.

If a drug is not almost unequivocally anaphrodisiac, like the opiates, expectations of sexual activity when it is used are likely to be self-ful-filling; that is often the case with cocaine. It is important that the drug is a luxury, used by many people only on special occasions. One can be-come intoxicated almost as fast on cheap red wine as on champagne, but champagne drinking is the form of alcohol consumption particularly as-sociated with romance. The use of cocaine by fashionable rich people and entertainers who are assumed to have particularly interesting sex lives has enhanced its reputation as an aphrodisiac.

Keeping all these important qualifications in mind, we can say that cocaine, like other stimulants, often heightens sexual interest and sexual powers in the short run. Interviews on drug use and sexual activity among patients at the Haight-Ashbury Free Medical Clinic in San Fran-cisco showed that these young people who used many different psy-choactive drugs often saved cocaine as a luxury for sexual occasions. Ten of the twenty men interviewed who had injected cocaine intravenously reported erections. Some also reported painful priapism, and one had ex-perienced multiple orgasms. Cocaine might also be used to anesthetize the penis and lengthen the time before ejaculation, and several women came to the clinic with the mucous membrane of the vagina inflamed from sexual intercourse under these conditions. The arterial vasodilator amyl nitrite ("poppers"), often used to heighten sensation at the moment of orgasm, was considered similar to cocaine but briefer and more intense in its effect. In another study, sailors at a navy drug rehabilitation center gave heightened sexual pleasure as their main reason for using cocaine: about a third of those described as light users and almost half of those de-scribed as heavy users took it to "get a sexual feeling" or to "improve sex-ual pleasure." Among other drugs, only cannabis was used for these pur-poses (alcohol was not included) and then by only a fifth of both light and heavy users. So, at least among dwellers on naval bases and in the Haight-Ashbury district, cocaine is a highly "sexual" drug. In Haight-Ashbury, but not on the naval base, amphetamines were also used for sexual purposes. They were explicitly given credit for greatly augmenting sex drive, "making chicks nymphos," causing men to "go all day and not

come," and instigating group sex. They also induced a fantasy state satis-
fied by casual sex contacts and occasionally caused erections in men and
orgasms in women when injected. Gay and Sheppard call amphetamine
"a true aphrodisiac." E. H. Ellinwood, in a study of amphetamine psychosis, also noted that the victims were often hypersexual: "The greatest
increase in libido was often noted in women and especially those who had
been relatively frigid prior to abusing amphetamines." [38]

The cocaine users we interviewed also reported sexual stimulation
commonly, though by no means universally. One said, "It's probably the
greatest aphrodisiac known." Another added, "If you're in a sexual situation . . . everything is delayed, so prior to orgasm, it may take three times
as long, and an orgasm is, like, expanded over a long period of time . . .
cocaine definitely not only heightens the act but increases the desire for
it, and generally does have all the qualities of a classical, good aphrodisiac." An opposite opinion was, "I heard other guys' stories, you know,
you shoot some coke, your sex desires go right to the top. It never affected
me that way." Still another interview subject commented, "You spend all
day snorting and making love and listening to music. . . . But I think you
can do some damage, because the body's like an astronaut, going on a
blastoff. 'Cause making love on cocaine, you don't know when to stop."
When asked whether he enjoyed sex more on cocaine, he said he did not.
Others said cocaine in small doses was somewhat aphrodisiac, but large
doses tended to make them lose interest. One man reported that "alcohol
makes you lustful, but sort of cloudy mentally, and cocaine makes you
lustful, but clear mentally." Another said that with large doses, "You can't
keep your mind on sex. You get beyond it. You get beyond most everything except the cocaine." Still another man said: "My senses were stimulated, but not sexually particularly." But we were also told that "If it is
an ego-boost for some people, it may be an ego-boost sexually as well."

Cocaine, like amphetamine, may apparently encourage a certain kind
of hard-driving sexuality in which the sexual act is a performance requir-
ing power and mastery. A recent doctoral thesis confirms, in a sense, the
reports of Gay's and Sheppard's subjects by showing experimentally that
cocaine and methamphetamine are the only ones among a wide variety of
psychoactive drugs that "improve" sexual performance in male rats as
measured by the number of ejaculations achieved in a given time. (High
doses of these drugs, however, are shown to inhibit sexual activity.) In a
recent Harold Robbins epic, a tireless black man, a lust-crazed white
woman, and an endless supply of cocaine and amyl nitrite are assumed to
be the perfect combination for best-selling sex.[39] Some Latin Americans
who use cocaine, and especially those who deal in it, are reported to

regard it as a *macho* drug that readies them for battle or sex at will. Cocaine is also supposedly used at what journalists call jet set orgies (where no doubt its sheer expense has almost as much allure as its psychopharmacological powers). The prolongation of sexual activity in men by the delay of ejaculation can also give a sense of power and control.

Many people consider cocaine to have the same special aphrodisiac effect on women that Ellinwood saw in amphetamine abusers. "Girl" and "lady" are a couple of the drug's aliases, possibly because men (and some women) believe that women love it. Early writers speak of the "nymphomania of cocainist women" [40] as some of the men interviewed by Gay and Sheppard spoke of the "nympho chicks" produced by amphetamines. One woman we interviewed said, "I've blown cocaine and had ecstatic sex. It's an aphrodisiac. . . . It's called 'the lady'; it brings out the most lady qualities in women. It makes you really feel incredibly feminine . . . coquetry . . . immediately, you do a little blow and you go and you put on your best clothes. . . . It brings out your artistry. In terms of lovemaking, very artistic lovemaking." Prostitutes commonly use it both to relieve fatigue and to make their work tolerable, if not enjoyable; it is said to be a popular accessory in high-priced brothels. One writer estimated that in 1913 half the prostitutes in Montmartre used it. [41] (At that time, of course, both prostitution and cocaine were legal in France.) Pimps have a reputation for keeping large supplies on hand. Like belladonna ("beautiful lady"), the source of the chemically related drug atropine, cocaine also dilates the pupils of the eyes and so makes women momentarily more attractive.

One of the men treated at Maier's clinic in Zürich in the 1920s gave him a particularly lurid account of the effect of cocaine on women. He believed that among habitual users it excited them sexually much more than it excited men, who were often psychologically aroused but unable to sustain an erection or come to a climax. He said that a little bit of cocaine made women insatiable and described orgies at "cocaine clubs" after which the participants felt remorseful and ashamed to look at one another. It is safe to assume that Maier's patient wanted to tell a good story and that Maier himself was prepared to associate an illicit drug with illicit sexual activity. Another student of cocaine use in the 1920s remarks that abusers' accounts of their sexual prowess and exploits are as dubious as their resolutions to renounce the drug and start a new life. A writer in *Playboy*, one of our own culturally approved sources of sexual connoisseurship, asserts, "Men consistently told me that women turn on for coke, but the women I talked to were vague on the subject." [42] Nevertheless, the testimony of Gay's and Sheppard's patients and the observations of Ellinwood on amphetamines suggest that the association of hypersexuality in women with the use of stimulants is more than just an expression of male fears or desires.

But people in general, and especially drug users, may have a tendency to magnify verbally the importance of sexuality and the sexual effects of drugs. Any drug, from amphetamine to barbiturate, that removes inhibitions may heighten erotic desires and fantasies. One of our society's standing joke topics is the use of alcohol to seduce women. Stimulants in particular may prolong and intensify sexual activity. But it is interesting to note that most of the people interviewed by Gay and Sheppard thought marihuana was the drug that most enhanced sexual pleasure, largely by reducing inhibitions and heightening sensibility without actually increasing sexual drive as stimulants may. And in the end, even among these drug sophisticates, "an almost invariable return to 'sex on the natch' [natural] is described." [43] Obviously the more spectacular sexual effects may come to seem undesirable, and once the novelty wears off, cannabis and other drugs often lose their apparent sexual powers.

Enhancement of sexual interest and capacity by cocaine, insofar as it exists, is in any case unreliable. L. Vervaeck, writing in 1923, found that only 20 to 30 percent of cocaine users became sexually excited and that stimulation often gave way to impotence and frigidity after a while. A number of the people we interviewed, including women, also reported no or only occasional sexual excitement. In spite of unreliable anecdotes about old coqueros with great sexual powers and some reports of erotic fantasies, there is little evidence that coca chewing has any significant aphrodisiac effect. Gutiérrez-Noriega says that the Indians rarely find it to be sexually stimulating. The women of the Kogi tribe, as we have mentioned, regard coca as a rival for the interest of the men rather than an ally of their own sexuality and desire for children. In large doses or after chronic consumption of substantial quantities, cocaine prevents at first ejaculation and later erection in men, even when erotic fantasy remains strong. In most of the cases of chronic cocaine abuse studied by Maier, the victims lost interest in sex after a few months.[44] Since people often go on using cocaine, as they go on using alcohol, long after the drug ceases to increase sexual interest or activity, the sexual effect is evidently not one of the most important reasons for using it. The effect of cocaine in this as in other respects may resemble that of an emergency situation. A suggestion of adventure or novelty may make sex more exciting for some members of the uncomfortably domesticated human species, but chronic stress makes it nearly impossible.

Acute Psychological Effects—Large Doses

The acute psychological effects of large or excessive doses of cocaine are strikingly similar to those of large doses of amphetamine. We will leave most of the discussion of the more severe symptoms of cocaine intoxication for Chapter 6, which deals with chronic use, because many of the phenomena associated with acute abuse do not appear until there has already been considerable chronic abuse, and the symptoms are often the same. But there may sometimes be serious acute effects, especially from injection, even before any chronic abuse. We have already spoken of the stereotyped behavior produced by both cocaine and the amphetamines. (Apparently its onset is slower with cocaine.) [45] This can take various forms, from minor chewing or teeth-grinding movements and unusual interest in tasks like sewing or typing to the absorption in apparently meaningless repetitive activities known as punding. Cocaine abuse, like amphetamine abuse, may also cause paranoia, ideas of reference, and delusions of grandeur.

A man we interviewed who had injected both cocaine and heroin intravenously described some paranoid episodes: "Cocaine will scare you, if it's strong enough. . . . I've had that experience, and the only way to bring that down is to shoot some heroin. . . . When I did get paranoid, I got paranoid about the police. I thought the police was after me. . . . You could walk down the street and turn the corner, and walk down the block half a block, and swear you hear somebody around the corner calling you, and you'll walk back, and turn the corner, and go back up the block . . . and there's nobody there." A man who sniffed rather than injected the drug reported this incident: "I was driving home, I stopped my car, I swear, and got out, walked to the back of the car, and peeped up the exhaust pipes, 'cause I thought somebody was in the car with me." Another comment from an interview was: "When I've shot a lot of coke— now I've shot coke for two or three hours, all night—I wake up in the morning and I come out—hey! think somebody behind me. . . . I know people that had been riding around town, thinkin' the police was after them . . . very seldom, I felt that way, paranoia. Only when I was over-doin' it, and *knew* I was overdoin' it." But none of the cocaine users we interviewed knew anyone who had experienced the kind of serious psychotic episode that, as we shall see in Chapter 6, is possible although not common.

In an 1889 article J. Chalmers da Costa describes "Four Cases of Cocaine Delirium" produced by application to the urethra or prepuce for surgical purposes. One man became pale and immobile, apparently ceased to breathe, and had an imperceptible pulse. His lips were pale and his face bathed in sweat. After 15 seconds shallow and slow breathing with a light pulse began, as unconsciousness and general insensibility to pain continued. Then his facial muscles twitched convulsively and he tossed his arms and legs. He began to talk incoherently, to laugh and sing, seemingly oblivious to his surroundings. As the delirium passed, he concentrated on his own ideas, which flowed torrentially and with intellectual brilliance. About an hour after the onset of the symptoms he fell asleep, waking two hours later with complaints of headache, giddiness, numbness of the extremities, and dryness of the throat. He repeated the urethral application on his own one night, and suffered severe after-effects including prostration, numbness, and dimness of vision. In another case the patient cried out after five minutes that he could not breathe, brushed imaginary bugs off his coat, and said that the physician was his brother. He staggered about like a drunken man, upset chairs, aimed blows at the doctor, and declared with distinct articulation that the doctor wanted to kill him. He was taken home and put to sleep with sodium bromide and morphine. In a third case the patient began to mutter a few minutes after application to the urethra and moved his hand as if sending a telegram (he was a telegraph operator). He talked about the need to send the message and "telegraphed" with great energy. After ten minutes he recovered, complained of difficulty in breathing, and had no memory of the immediately preceding period. The next morning he felt dull and heavy for a few hours.[46]

Acute Physiological Effects—Moderate and Excessive Doses

The unequivocally physiological effects of cocaine are as a rule not nearly so important as the psychological ones. We have already mentioned most of them or referred to them by implication. If cocaine is sniffed it produces a cold or numb sensation in the nose and palate; taken nasally or orally it anesthetizes the taste buds. Otherwise, the physiological phenomena it causes are characteristic of sympathetic excitement. It increases the basal metabolic rate and produces hyperglycemia (a heightened level of blood sugar), an increase in muscle tone, and mydriasis (dilation of the pupil of the eye); it also constricts peripheral blood vessels. The throat often becomes dry, and stomach and intestinal activity is usually reduced. (Freud, drinking 50 mg in a 1 percent solution, reports a "cooling eructation.") Cocaine also makes breathing faster and deeper and increases the heart rate, although it may sometimes slow the heart momentarily at first by central stimulation of the vagus nerve. It raises body temperature and sometimes induces sweating; men who chew coca often say that it makes them feel warm. In a group experimentally exposed to cold, those who were chewing coca showed a slower core temperature decline and a quicker decline of temperature in the extremities (because of peripheral vasoconstriction). The hyperthermia (temperature elevation) is primarily a central rather than a peripheral effect, since it does not occur in animals under general anesthesia. It is not related to muscular activity, since it appears even in animals prevented from moving. Probably the thermal regulator mechanism in the hypothalamus is affected directly.[47]

At larger doses, especially intravenous or subcutaneous, cocaine can produce headache, pallor, cold sweat, rapid and weak pulse, tremors, Cheyne-Stokes respiration (fast, irregular, and shallow), nausea, vertigo, convulsions, unconsciousness, and death. Most people who take large doses, including several men we interviewed, are frightened by the pounding of their hearts and likely to believe that death, if it occurred, would be from cardiovascular collapse. It is true that if a large amount of cocaine enters the body very rapidly (i.e., by intravenous injection) there may be an idiosyncratic direct toxic effect on the cardiac muscle that causes it to stop beating, usually after ventricular fibrillation (rapid twitching of individual fibers or small bundles of fibers in the ventricle of the heart). But paralysis of the medullary brain center that controls respiration, often preceded by convulsions, is the most common cause of death.[48]

Incidence of Death and Acute Poisoning

The lethal dose is uncertain and variable. According to Gutiérrez-Noriega and Zapata Ortiz, in dogs it is 20 mg per kg orally (about 1.4 grams for a 150-pound man) or 10 to 12 mg per kg subcutaneously or intravenously (about 700 to 850 mg in a 150-pound man). They claim that the safety margin is low, because the lethal dose may be only twice the optimum stimulant dose. But William Hammond, as we shall see, took

800 mg and 1.2 grams subcutaneously on two occasions (the latter, admittedly, in four doses over a 20-minute period). Although both these quantities exceed the dose estimated to be lethal by Gutiérrez-Noriega and Zapata Ortiz, he suffered no permanent ill effects. Reliable information on this subject is very hard to come by, but as little as 20 mg applied to the nasal mucous membrane or 1.2 grams taken orally is supposed to have caused death in unusual cases; this is probably a rare anaphylactoid effect.[49]

In the first 40 or 50 years of cocaine use there were many reports of acute poisoning and sometimes death, usually in surgery. One of the earliest of these is J. B. Mattison's 1891 article, "Cocaine Poisoning." From the period 1888 to 1891 he recounts six deaths and a number of other cases of acute poisoning. He refers to other fatalities and poisonings totaling over 200 recorded cases and suggests that still more have gone unreported. He advises great caution in the use of "this peerless drug" with its highly uncertain lethal dose. To cite one of his cases:

> Male, age 29, one drachm [a teaspoonful] of a 20 per cent solution injected in urethra, prior to urethrotomy. Instrument was scarcely removed, when patient made a foolish remark, facial muscles twitched, eyes staring, frothed at mouth, and face was congested, breathing embarrassed and a violent epileptiform convulsion, lasting several seconds, ensued. This, increasingly severe, continued several times a minute; the whole muscular system was involved, requiring force to keep him on table. Lung action first failed, then the heart irregular and slow, breathing more and more disturbed, face and entire body deeply congested, and twenty minutes from the first convulsion, patient was dead.

This was a large dose, nearly 800 mg. Other deaths came from injections into the eyelid (three-quarters of a syringe [of unspecified size] of 5 percent solution), breast (225 mg), and gums (1 gram), or large amounts—about a gram and a half—taken by mouth. In an incident that was not fatal, "Would-be suicide took 22 grains [about 1.5 grams] in beer, causing great belly pain, intense dyspnoea and vertigo, and urine suppression for 24 hours." Another example: "J. Chalmers da Costa reported to me the case of woman, age 22, in whose forehead he injected 10 min. [a minim is one-sixtieth of a teaspoon, or about one drop] of a 6 percent solution [only about 60 mg of cocaine], causing shallow, rapid breathing, quick, weak pulse, great tremor, temperature 102, with delirium for several hours, and complete analgesia." [50]

In a report in the *Journal of the American Medical Association* for 1924 on "The Toxic Effects Following the Use of Local Anesthetics," Emil Mayer analyzes 43 fatalities. Although by that time procaine was being used far more than any other local anesthetic, cocaine caused 26 of the deaths, usually by producing convulsions and respiratory failure a few minutes after its application. The most dangerous sites and techniques of administration were applications to the inflamed urethra and to the tonsils (mostly for tonsillectomy). The accidental substitution of cocaine for procaine caused two deaths. The committee headed by Mayer recommended that cocaine not be injected into the submucous tissue or subcutaneously and also that only solutions of low concentration be used on skin and mucous surfaces. It opposed the use of cocaine paste or "mud" as a preoperative measure.[51]

It is as difficult to say how common acute poisoning or death from cocaine was or is as to say what dose is lethal. Deaths in surgery now occur very seldom, since surgeons now use the drug less often and more cautiously. One exception is a case recently reported in the journal *Anesthesia and Analgesia*. In preparation for a bronchogram to determine lung pathology, a physician in a medical clinic administered a 10 percent solution of cocaine to the throat and trachea by mistake instead of the correct 1 percent solution. The patient, a 22-year-old woman, suffered a cardiac arrest which produced permanent brain damage and has been in a coma since June 1972. She has been awarded $2,000,000 in damages from the clinic and the pharmacy that supplied the drug, an amount said to be the largest ever awarded to one person in a malpractice suit. Deaths from recreational use have probably always been rare, and sniffing in particular rarely causes serious acute poisoning. For example, in a 1920 article based on the records of the New York City Narcotic Clinic, S. Dana Hubbard cites only one recorded death in 1919 from cocaine and 51 from opiates. Statistics from the City and County Coroner's Office of San Francisco in 1973 show 80 deaths from heroin, 137 deaths from barbiturates, 553 deaths from alcohol, 10 deaths from amphetamines, and none at all from cocaine. (There were two in 1971–1972.) A 1974 article in the *New York Times* on the East Side singles scene reported the death of a young woman in a Times Square hotel from what appeared on autopsy to be an overdose of cocaine. But the article states that medical examiners and police believe cocaine deaths to be rare and therefore suspect murder in that case.[52]

These very low numbers may be misleading. Deaths from cocaine may simply not have been recognized in the past, because large-scale cocaine users almost always take other drugs that are more familiar to the authorities, and cocaine use comes to the attention of the law and physicians less often than, say, opiates, because of the absence of a physiological need for the drug. Also, cocaine is metabolized quickly and therefore difficult to detect in the blood or urine. Official attributions of cause of death are often influenced by socially accepted myths; for example, it is now recognized that many of the deaths once attributed to heroin overdose were probably caused by a combination of heroin with alcohol or barbiturates, by alcohol and barbiturates alone, or even by the quinine used to cut most street heroin. A recent experiment on mice is especially interesting in this respect. It indicates that the LD 50 (dose that kills half the experimental population) of heroin is 57 mg per kg, of quinine 138 mg per kg, and of cocaine 31 mg per kg, all intravenously. The LD 50 of heroin is raised by small proportions of cocaine but actually lowered by large proportions. R. D. Pickett, who conducted the experiment, believes that in the doses usually used by heroin addicts (equal proportions by weight of the two drugs) cocaine potentiates heroin's lethal effect.[53] The tendency of a large amount of cocaine to paralyze the respiratory center in the brain may be supplementing the respiratory depression produced by opiates. The LD 50 of cocaine alone in this experiment was the equivalent of about two grams intravenously in a 150-pound man, far more than most people ever use; but human beings are probably more susceptible than mice to the drug, and may become more sensitive to its toxic effects as they continue to use it. Whatever we make of these results, it is possible that as cocaine is used more often and becomes more prominent in the public consciousness, more deaths will be attributed to it, either truly or falsely. Certainly as long as the law continues to treat the drug as it does now, practically everyone will have an interest in obscuring the truth and confusing the issue in one way or another.

Deaths from recreational use, then, may not be so rare as they seem, at least if the drug is injected rather than sniffed. As Maier observed in 1926, death by cocaine poisoning may be attributed to "heart attack" if no tests are made for chemicals in the blood. Autopsy after an overdose usually shows hyperemia (congestion with blood) of the brain, lungs, liver, and kidneys. There may also be fatty degeneration of liver cells and lung infarctions (necrosis of tissue) produced by embolisms (obstructions of blood flow) formed because of the slowing of capillary circulation by peripheral vasoconstriction. But these phenomena are not diagnostically specific for cocaine poisoning. Maier was convinced that three of his former patients' "heart attacks" were deaths from cocaine. If fatalities occurred even in surgery, when immediate help was usually available, they must have occurred in other situations too and gone unreported or misreported out of fear of the law.[54]

In the 1920s it was commonly accepted that an overdose of cocaine could be lethal, and sometimes the drug was used in suicide attempts like the one described by Mattison. Vervaeck recounts several cases of suicide by cocaine; one was a London dancer who died after swallowing at least 500 mg. In Jean Cocteau's novel *Le grand écart* (*The Big Split*), published in 1923, the hero, after hearing about a man who died from "sniffing too much powder," tries to commit suicide by drinking whiskey containing ten grams of cocaine. He survives only because the bartender who sells him the drug swindles him by diluting it. Cocteau had used cocaine and other drugs himself and probably knew what he was talking about when he implied that one could die from sniffing cocaine, although he may have been thinking of the complications of chronic abuse rather than acute overdose.[55]

Nonfatal incidents of acute poisoning from recreational use of cocaine are easier to document. A man we interviewed recounted one: "I stopped shooting it. I've shot it once since I was 20, and it was a disaster. . . . I took too much, and I felt as though my head was going to explode. I was sick for about 12 hours, and I puked for about three hours. My friends kept telling me to go to bed. Later they told me I was moaning all night, loudly, and I didn't know it. My body was in complete agony, and there was no relief. That was the last time I shot it." Another interview subject described ill effects from excessive snorting: "I've had too much coke, and I've felt, you know, for like an hour, all the traditional things you're supposed to feel when overdosing, crawling like bugs in your skin, really hot sweat, nausea, and just feeling like you're almost dying, for almost 15 minutes." In another incident, an interview subject who had sniffed two-thirds of a gram in a short period of time (she is not sure whether the cocaine was cut with other drugs) felt this effect: "It seemed like I was going to pass out any second . . . a very dead feeling in my whole body, but my heart racing. . . . I was afraid of my heart giving out. . . . I was aware that taking that much was self-destructive; I felt it was sort of suicidal. I had no idea how much it took to o.d. . . . Since that experience, I've dropped off. I became more conscious of the heartbeat speeding, paranoia kinds of effects." Although incidents like these may become more common as cocaine becomes more popular, they are probably unusual now. If a recent DEA survey can be trusted, cocaine overdoses rarely bring people to the emergency rooms of hospitals.[56]

The basic treatment for cocaine overdose is revival of breathing by artificial respiration or administration of oxygen under pressure, facilitated if necessary by a muscle relaxant like diazepam or even succinylcholine. If convulsions occur, a short-acting barbiturate like sodium pentothal intravenously in small doses (25–50 mg) is recommended. One clinical toxicologist suggests 1 to 2 mg intravenously of propanolol (a drug that blocks catecholamine receptors in the peripheral nervous system) and 1 mg physostigmine intramuscularly, or else 200 mg oral secobarbital. A heart stimulant like phenylephrine or cardiac massage may be necessary. Action must be taken very quickly, because death usually arrives in less than five minutes and rarely takes as much as half an hour. If the patient survives this early period he or she will probably recover fully.[57]

Postscript: Report of an Experiment

William A. Hammond (1828–1900) was Surgeon General of the United States Army during the Civil War and later became an enthusiastic advocate of the use of cocaine. He left an eloquent and detailed report of an experiment on himself that he undertook in 1885 to determine the effects of different doses of the drug.[58] Of course, his testimony lacks all statistical virtues and even the experimental virtues of controls and double-blindness, but in the absence of any substantial information of this kind about the effects of cocaine on human beings (Offerman's experiment is a partial exception), what Hammond has to say is of great interest:

I began by injecting a grain [65 mg] of the substance under the skin of the forearm, the operation being performed at 8 o'clock P.M. The first effect ensued in about five minutes, and consisted of a pleasant thrill which seemed to pass through the whole body. . . . On feeling the pulse five minutes after making the injection, it was found to be 94, while immediately before the operation it was only 82. With these physical phenomena there was a sense of exhilaration and an increase of mental activity that were marked, and not unlike in character those that ordinarily follow a glass or two of champagne. I was writing at the time, and I found that my thoughts flowed with increased freedom and were unusually well expressed. The influence was felt for two hours, when it gradually began to fade. At 12 o'clock (four hours after the injection) I went to bed, feeling, however, no disposition to sleep. I lay awake till daylight, my mind actively going over all the events of the previous day. When I at last fell asleep it was only for two or three hours, and then I awoke with a severe frontal headache. This passed off after breakfast.

On the second night following, at 7 o'clock, I injected *two grains*. . . . All the phenomena attendant on the first experiment were present in this, and to an increased degree. In addition there were twitching of the muscles of the face, and a slight tremor of the hands noticed especially in writing. . . . I felt a great desire to write, and did so with a freedom and apparent clearness that astonished me . . . when I came to peruse it . . . it was entirely coherent, logical, and as good if not better in general character as anything I had previously written. The effects of this dose did not disappear till the middle of the next day, nor until I had drunk two or three cups of strong coffee. I slept little or none at all, the night being passed in tossing from side to side of the bed, and in thinking of the most preposterous subjects. . . . Four nights subsequently I injected *four grains* [260 mg] of the hydrochlorate of cocaine into the skin of the left forearm. The effects were similar in almost every respect with those of the other experiments except that they were much more intense. . . . I wrote page after page, throwing the sheets on the floor without stopping to gather them together. When, however, I came to look them over on the following morning, I found that I had written a series of high-flown sentences altogether different from my usual style, and bearing upon matters in which I was not in the least interested . . . and yet it appeared to me at the time that what I was writing consisted of ideas of very superior character. . . .

The disturbance of the action of the heart was also exceedingly well marked, and may be described best by the word "tumultuous." At times, beginning within three minutes after the injection, and continuing with more or less intensity all through the night, the heart beat so rapidly that its pulsations could not be counted, and then its action would suddenly fall to a rate not exceeding 60 in a minute, every now and then dropping a beat. This irregularity was accompanied by a disturbance of respiration of a similar character, and by a sense of oppression in the chest that added greatly to my discomfort.

On subsequent nights I took *six, eight, ten, and twelve grains* of the cocaine at a dose. . . . The effects . . . were similar in general characteristics though of gradually increasing intensity. . . . In one, that in which *twelve grains* [780 mg] were taken, I was conscious of a tendency to talk, and as far as my recollection extends, I believe I did make a long speech on some subject of which I had no remembrance the next day. . . . Insomnia was a marked characteristic, and there was invariably a headache the following morning. In all cases, however, the effects passed off about midday. . . . A consideration of the phenomena observed appeared to show that the effects produced by twelve grains were not very much more pronounced than those following six grains. I determined, therefore, to make one more experiment, and to inject *eighteen grains* [1170 mg]. . . .

I had taken the doses of eight, ten, and twelve grains in divided quantities, and this dose of eighteen grains I took in four portions within five minutes of each other. At once an effect was produced upon the heart, and before I had taken the last injection the pulsations were 140 to the minute and characteristically irregular. In all the former experiments, although there was great mental exaltation, amounting at times almost to delirium, it was nevertheless distinctly under my control. . . . But in this instance, within five minutes after taking the last injection, I felt that my mind was passing beyond my control, and that I was becoming an irresponsible agent. I did not feel exactly in a reckless mood, but I was in such a frame of mind as to be utterly regardless of any calamity or danger that might be impending over me. . . . I lost consciousness of all my acts within, I think, half an hour after finishing the administration of the dose. Probably, however, other moods supervened, for the next day when I came downstairs, three hours after my usual time, I found the floor of my library strewn with encyclopaedias, dictionaries, and other books of reference, and one or two chairs overturned. I certainly was possessed of the power of mental and physical action in accordance with the ideas by which I was governed, for I had turned out the gas in the room and gone upstairs to my bed-chamber and lighted the gas, and put the match used in a safe place, and undressed, laying my clothes in their usual place, had cleaned my teeth and gone to bed. Doubtless these acts were all automatic, for I had done them all in pretty much the same way for a number of years. During the night the condition which existed was, judging from the previous experiments, certainly not sleep; and yet I remained entirely unconscious until 9 o'clock the following morning, when I found myself in bed with a splitting headache and a good deal of cardiac and respiratory disturbance. For several days afterward I felt the effects of this extreme dose in a certain degree of languor and indisposition to mental or physical exertion; there was also a difficulty in concentrating the attention, but I slept soundly every night without any notable disturbance from dreams. . . .

Certainly in this instance I came very near taking a fatal dose, and I would not advise anybody to repeat the experiment. . . .

It is surprising that no marked influence appeared to be exercised upon the spinal cord or upon the ganglia at the base of the brain. Thus there were no disturbances of sensibility (no anaesthesia) and no interference with motility, except that some of the muscles, especially those of the face, were subjected to slight twitchings. In regard to sight and hearing, I noticed that both were affected, but that while the sharpness of vision was decidedly lessened, the hearing was increased in acuteness. At no time were there any hallucinations.

6

EFFECTS OF CHRONIC

USE

THE JUSTIFICATION for outlawing cocaine was mainly the supposed psychological and physiological consequences of prolonged use. But the law does not distinguish, as we must, between moderate and excessive doses. The more spectacular consequences of cocaine abuse are not typical of the drug's effects as it is normally used any more than the phenomena associated with alcoholism are typical of the ordinary consumption of that drug. We insist on this here because we may seem to be overemphasizing the most harmful effects, and we do not want to imply that it is impossible to use cocaine (or any other drug) in moderation. If we seem to speak about severe abuse at too great length, it is because this is more important to the user and society than the occasional Saturday night "blow," just as alcoholism is more important than ordinary social drinking. The question of how often cocaine or any other drug will in fact be abused, or used at all, is quite different from the issue of the effects of its abuse. It involves a number of conditions, including above all availability, that conspire to create what is called drug dependence or a drug habit. This is largely a social and cultural phenomenon, which we shall discuss more fully in Chapter 8.

Effects of Chronic Coca Use

⟨The best source of information, inadequate as it is, on the long-term effects of moderate doses of cocaine is studies of the coca-chewing regions of South America⟩ The anecdotal evidence, from the time of the Spanish conquest on, is unfortunately variable, unreliable, contradictory, and heavily colored by the biases of the observers.⟨We are told on the one hand that *coqueros* are liars, depraved, pickpockets, indolent, submissive, depressed, stupid, and subject to muscular degeneration, anemia, jaundiced skin, digestive complaints, and other diseases; and on the other hand that coca is a harmless stimulant and tonic which has never caused any nervous or physical disease.⟩ Poeppig believed that habitual use of coca caused mental and physical decadence, but Mantegazza, Tschudi, and others considered it healthful in moderation and rarely overused. Richard E. Schultes told us that the members of the Yucuña tribe in the Amazon region of Colombia, the largest consumers of coca he had ever encountered, were also remarkably strong and healthy. He doubts that misery and malnutrition among the highland Indians has much to do with coca.

Gutiérrez-Noriega and Zapata Ortiz undertook the first serious systematic studies of the chronic psychological and physiological effects of coca chewing. In spite of their conviction that the habit was dangerous, the results have to be called inconclusive. In a 1947 study, "Mental Alterations Produced by Coca," Gutiérrez-Noriega asserts that *coqueros* who chew 20 to 50 grams of leaves a day are very much like non-*coqueros* matched for relevant variables. But those who chew over 100 grams a day, he says, are very different: they are dull and torpid, sit silent and motionless for hours, have dry skin and bad posture, lack sexual interest, answer questions vaguely, make contradictory statements, and cannot handle abstract ideas. Gutiérrez-Noriega believes that the women, who do not chew coca, are more intelligent and energetic. He also comments that most people in the area he studied believe that coca is good for health. He admits that the apathy, timidity, and introversion found in some *coqueros* is an accentuation of the Andean temperament that apparently existed even before the Spanish arrived and consumption of coca became common. But he concludes that "There is no medical problem of greater importance in Peru." In another article Gutiérrez-Noriega and Zapata Ortiz note that illiteracy is highest where coca chewing is most common, but they also note that these are the areas where Quechua is spoken instead of Spanish. They admit that most *coqueros* show no obvious personality or mental deterioration, and the only abstinence symptoms they found were occasional depression and irritability.[1]

Gutiérrez-Noriega and Zapata Ortiz also studied "Intelligence and Personality in Persons Habituated to Coca." They found subnormal intelligence on the Binet and Porteus Maze tests and a longer reaction time to sound stimuli than in non-*coqueros*. The longer a *coquero* had been chewing, the lower his scores were. On the Rohrschach test *coqueros* produced fewer total responses, fewer global responses, and fewer original ideas than controls. The Rohrschach results revealed personalities described as apathetic, indolent, and hypoaffective. Gutiérrez-Noriega and Zapata Ortiz concluded that chronic intoxication by coca was a major cause of intellectual deterioration.[2] This study was conducted in Lima, where *coqueros* are a deviant minority, and it has been criticized for this reason.

J. C. Negrete and H. B. M. Murphy have made the most carefully controlled study of this topic. In an analysis, "Psychological Deficit in Chewers of Coca Leaf," they chose as their subjects 50 *coqueros* and 42 controls who worked in the fields on a sugar plantation in northern Argentina. All were men between the ages of 25 and 49; about half were Bolivian migrant workers and half local residents; half were literate and half illiterate; and half were older than 36. This location was chosen because neither men who chewed coca (as in Lima) nor those who did not chew it (as in some areas of the Peruvian and Bolivian Andes) were considered a deviant minority, and the population was more or less equally divided between chewers and nonchewers. Negrete and Murphy eliminated anyone with a history of mental disorder, head injury, epilepsy, physical illnesses known to affect mental functioning, "erratic or antisocial work practices," or excessive drinking. The exclusion of heavy drinkers, they say, biased the sample so that the controls were slightly younger and more literate than the chewers; but they believe the sample remained satisfactory. A chewer was defined as someone who had chewed 200 grams a week for at least ten years. The men used as controls were never seen to use coca while working and denied having taken more than an average of 10 grams a week.

Noting the fact that chronic users were often said to look dull and apathetic, Negrete and Murphy used a battery of tests designed to measure psychological deficit caused by organic brain damage. They admit that there is no single reliable method of measuring this and that the concept of brain damage is a very loose one. They also point out that there is no evidence of damage by the coca alkaloids to any specific part of the brain. The battery of tests included a verbal intelligence scale, auditory and visual memory tests, figure completion and similarity recognition tests from the Army Beta scale, an attention test (the Knox cubes), a test of manual ability, tactile and spatial memory, and learning (the Seguin Form Board test), and a block design test adapted from Wechsler. Although the examiner knew whether each individual was a chewer or a control, Negrete and Murphy believe that examiner bias had no influence, since the researchers did not expect to find a difference between the two groups.

When allowances were made for age, literacy, and background (local or immigrant), the *coqueros* performed worse than the controls in almost all respects. Only the verbal intelligence test yielded no significant differences; the researchers expected this from previous work on brain damage. The differences were greatest on the Army Beta tests and the learning measure of the sorting test (Seguin Form Board). The researchers asked about diet but found no reason to suspect greater dietary deficiencies among the chewers. (It is not clear how thoroughly they examined this question.) They reject the suggestion that men who take up the habitual use of coca are deficient to start with. First, they believe, a lower native intelligence would have shown up most clearly on the verbal intelligence scale. Second, they found a relationship between duration of chewing, apart from age, and four of the test scores (auditory memory, manual learning, and immediate and delayed attention). Temporary intoxication did not seem to affect the results: there was no correlation between lower test scores and recent large doses. Negrete and Murphy reject the hypothesis that chronic use of coca induces retardation or depression by exciting inhibitory reflexes, because chewers took no longer on the tests than controls. They conclude, however, that "coca must be assumed to have an adverse effect on the brain until it is proved otherwise." Still, the deficiencies revealed by the tests were not observable on casual inspection or even during the test taking; the authors believed they would remain unimportant as long as *coqueros* lacked social opportunities to make use of their intelligence.[3]

In a later study Murphy, O. Rios, and Negrete tried to determine whether long-term coca use would in fact prevent *coqueros* from learning new skills if the occasion arose. Working in the same sugar-growing area of northern Argentina and with a similar population, they admitted 20 chewers and 10 controls to the empty wing of a plantation hospital for ten days. Of the chewers, 10 were supplied with their customary amount of coca and 10 were required to abstain. Abstainers tolerated the absence of the drug easily, and some of them said they would not have used it in such circumstances anyway, since its purpose was to suppress hunger and fatigue. They were more annoyed about the enforced abstention from alcohol. All the subjects took repeatedly, at intervals of three days, a single battery of tests consisting of the items in the previous study by Negrete and Murphy that had distinguished best between coca users and controls: the auditory memory test, the Army Beta tests, the attention test, the Seguin Form Board, and some of the block design tests.

Assuming a chronic psychological deficit of some kind, one could expect *coqueros* to score worse initially and perhaps improve less than controls. If the immediate effect of coca compensated for some of the chronic damage, the continuing users should score better than the abstainers. Finally, if there was a strong withdrawal reaction, the scores of the abstainers, especially on attention tests, might be expected to decline. The results showed no substantial effects of recent consumption or withdrawal. All three groups improved on each test in approximately equal degrees from the first to the third trial. The subtests on which the continuing users improved most compared with the other groups were ones that required manual dexterity rather than memorizing or abstract thinking. On the memory and attention tests, literate controls scored much higher than illiterate ones, while literate *coqueros* performed no better than illiterate ones. The authors suggest that there is a kind of memory developed by formal training in school and destroyed by chronic consumption of coca.

From a detailed analysis of the tests, the authors conclude that chronic coca use does not affect simple untrained memory, hand-mind coordination, or elementary concept formation. *Coqueros* showed no clinical signs of ataxia or poor muscle control, and the tests revealed no language difficulties or perception disturbances that suggested damage to a particular area of the brain. The coca users fell behind most on memorizing associated with literacy and on the more difficult abstract sections of the Army Beta subtests. They found it easy to compare figures to which they could give a name but hard to compare, say, geometric designs. The authors believe that the failures of the *coqueros* have a common source in a deficiency in abstract thinking of the kind found in some lobotomized patients and patients with lesions of the frontal lobes and possibly related to extensive loss of brain tissue in any lobe. Kurt Goldstein's description of this kind of patient, according to the authors, resembles the accounts that have sometimes been given of heavy coca users in the high Andes. They conclude that older *coqueros* might find it difficult to grasp the principles behind innovations in social organization but would have no trouble understanding and using new techniques in farming and industry presented in sufficiently concrete form. Since the present conditions of their lives do not permit abstract thinking, coca is probably doing as much good as harm. For the time being, the authors believe, efforts should be devoted to social reform rather than eradicating the habit.[4]

The test results may in fact be more ambiguous and inconclusive than Negrete, Murphy, and Rios think. The basic question, of course, is whether the relationship between coca use and test scores is causal. A subsidiary issue is the precise meaning of the capacities supposedly measured by the tests. First, there are problems of bias in the sample. By excluding excessive drinkers and men with erratic work practices, the authors may have weighted the coca-using group with subjects whose prior intellectual or psychological deficiencies would have caused alcoholism or inability to work regularly if they had not taken to chewing coca instead. The question of diet was not examined closely, either; other research, as we shall see, suggests that malnutrition is a major cause of coca chewing. As for the tests themselves, the authors rely heavily on the hypothesis that verbal intelligence (on which *coqueros* and controls scored the same) is less easily impaired by organic brain damage than the capacities measured by the Army Beta figure completion and similarity recognition tests (on which *coqueros* scored lower). In rejecting the contention that the coca users in their sample were less intelligent than the controls to begin with, Negrete and Murphy mention an association between duration of chewing and certain test scores. But these scores do *not* include the abstract sections of the Army Beta tests, supposed to be the best measure of a deficiency in abstract thinking associated with chronic brain damage. In any case, it is also possible that whatever environmental or physiological conditions cause a man to keep chewing coca also cause progressive deterioration in performance on some of the tests. In short, confusing environmental variables and difficulties in interpreting the tests make the results of the work by Negrete, Murphy, and Rios less conclusive than they might hope.

Working in conjunction with Murphy and Negrete, D. Goddard, S. N. de Goddard, and P. C. Whitehead conducted a study, "Social Factors Associated with Coca Use in the Andean Region," in the same area and using the same criteria for admission to the sample. The subjects were 58 of Negrete's and Murphy's respondents and 20 others: 40 users and 38 controls. In the region studied it was regarded as natural to use coca but no stigma was attached to not using it. Coca was chewed "to avoid sleep, to get a will to work, to have willingness to work, not to work better," and also sometimes to provide physical strength for heavy labor and courage to face dangers like snakebite and accidents. It was said to make the step lighter and to quench thirst in hot weather. The workers rarely invested coca with curative or magical powers, although some thought it good for stomach pains. Some subjects in both the *coquero* and control groups considered coca a mild vice, but the drug had no effect on the organization of social life. The attitudes of the nonusers toward coca were classified as one-third negative, one-third indifferent, and one-third favorable. But no one felt very strongly about it. The use of coca by women was not disapproved, and 28 percent of the total sample had wives who sometimes chewed it, mostly in gatherings with friends or while doing the laundry or other household tasks.

In this study the effect of coca on children, family life, and social activity was also examined. From fragmentary evidence, the authors conclude that coca chewing by parents has no adverse effect on children's school performance. Teachers thought that coca use among older children made little difference except that the chewers might be slightly more alert. Adult *coqueros* did not have lower aspirations for themselves or their children than adult controls, and *coqueros* showed neither more nor less social isolation than controls. The authors conclude that coca chewing in the Andes does not define or restrict social relationships; it is very much like the use of gum, tobacco, betel nut, or alcohol elsewhere. They do not mention the resemblance to the use of coffee and tea, which is even greater.[5]

The methodological difficulties in showing a causal relationship between coca chewing and organic deterioration are almost as great as those of showing a relationship to psychological damage. Gutiérrez-Noriega and Zapata Ortiz, studying 500 *coqueros* in 1948, found many constitutional disturbances and signs of degeneration: anemia, eye disease, caries, hepatomegaly, muscle weakness, hyperthyroidism, and so on.[6] But very little can be proved without controls; it is hardly surprising that these conditions afflict undernourished peasants with practically no access to physicians. In 1968 Alfred A. Buck and his colleagues made a controlled study of the correlation between coca chewing and various measures of physical health among residents of a Peruvian village. The village, population 492, was at an altitude of 2,400 feet and its climate was humid and tropical. Quechua Indians, migrants from the high Andes, made up 23 percent of the population; the rest were *mestizos*. Of the 53 coca chewers in the village, 28 were Quechuas and 25 *mestizos*. Fifty-one of the coca chewers were matched with controls of the same sex, ethnic group, and approximate age; medical information was obtained by interviews, physical examinations, laboratory tests, and skin tests. Three hypotheses were tested: that coca causes malnutrition by diminishing the sensation of hunger; that it produces indifference to personal hygiene; and that the work performance of *coqueros* is inferior (presumably for reasons of organic dysfunction).

As measures of nutritional state, weight-height ratio, skinfold thickness on the back and upper arms (a measure of subcutaneous fat), and serum albumin level were examined. There were statistically significant differences favoring the controls on the last two measures. The indicators of personal hygiene used were prevalence of scabies and pyodermia (skin infections), prevalence of intestinal parasites in stool specimens, and frequency of reported rat bites. Only in the prevalence of pyodermia was there a statistically significant difference in favor of the controls. Fewer coca chewers were infested with amoebae, and the authors wonder whether coca leaves have amoebicidal properties. (Cocaine does have a paralytic effect on lower organisms, and in one instance reported to us it seemed to relieve amoebic dysentery.) To test work performance effects, the researchers asked each subject how many work days he had lost because of illness in the preceding month. The average was almost twice as many days for the coca chewers as for the controls. Coca chewers had more often suffered severe anemia, and their hemoglobin levels were significantly lower in all weight-height categories. Hepatomegaly (enlarged liver) was twice as common among *coqueros* as among controls. The authors conclude that under the conditions of their study, habitual coca chewing is associated with poor health.

But they admit: "The directions and sequences of causes and effects cannot be identified clearly, because the conditions recognized by the study as possible disease determinants are arranged in a vicious circle." Difficulties were also created by the choice of a village in which only a small minority of the population chewed coca and the attempt to compensate by matching techniques. As the authors note, there were significantly more Protestants in the control groups, since the Evangelical mission in the village did not condone the use of coca, tobacco, or alcohol. In fact, two-thirds of the Quechua controls were Protestant (and, of course, none of the *coqueros* were). But conversion from traditional Catholicism to Protestant Evangelism in such a village must imply differences in native disposition or changes in attitudes toward work and hygiene that would be overwhelmingly more important than the effects of chewing coca. In this case, giving up coca was a symbolic act representing a decision for a new way of life. In general, matching techniques are unreliable, since matching for some variables may cause the groups to be dissimilar in respect to more important ones. The very fact that each control was of the same age, sex, and ethnic group as the corresponding coca chewer makes us wonder why one used coca and the other did not; the answer to this question, as we have pointed out in the case of the Protestants, may be far more significant than any consequence of the use of coca itself.[7]

In a further study of possible physiological effects, James E. Hamner III and Oscar L. Villegas examined the cheeks of coca chewers for signs of cancer. They did biopsies of 36 tin miners and found that the mucous membranes were swollen, gray-white, and opaque, but without signs of carcinoma or chronic ulcer. They noted the betel-nut chewing in southern Asia, with or without added tobacco, was highly correlated with oral cancer, but that oral cancer was rare in Bolivia and Peru. They concluded that the condition they observed was not premalignant.[8]

The evidence associating coca use with minor deficiences in mental and physical health or intellect is convincing (at least for the Andes and their foothills—anecdotal reports from Colombia and the Amazon give a different impression), but the causal connection has not been established. If coca users are thin, or their standards of hygiene are low, or they suffer more from minor illnesses and accidents, or they cannot handle abstractions and sometimes seem demoralized, that is easy to understand from many circumstances of their lives. It is likely that the men who suffer most from personal inadequacies and oppressive social conditions turn to the drug for solace. They also turn to alcohol. The connection between coca use and alcoholism is especially interesting. Gutiérrez-Noriega asserts that "the alcoholism that generally accompanies cocaism" makes it difficult to isolate the effects of coca. The United Nations Commission notes that observers in the Andes often say that alcohol is a far more serious problem than coca.[9] In all the studies we have discussed, adjusting for the probable effects of alcohol has been a problem. Any study that includes heavy or excessive drinkers is likely to confound the effects of alcohol with those of coca, and any study that deliberately excludes them is unavoidably creating a biased sample. Since some of the same conditions that drive men to use alcohol may drive them to use coca, *coqueros* deprived of their drug might replace it with alcohol.

Alcohol is only one of the many variables in this situation which may or may not be mere nuisances to be factored out. Probably the most important is poor nutrition, which is obviously a source of physical deficiencies and probably also associated with low scores on intelligence tests, poor work performance, and carelessness about personal hygiene. The trouble is that it has not been determined whether the use of coca is a cause or an effect of dietary deficiency, or neither, or both. According to a report by Zapata Ortiz on a brief experiment in the Peruvian Andes, *coqueros* gave up the drug when their nutrition was improved. Zapata Ortiz also points out that Indians tend to stop using coca when they join the Peruvian army, which provides them with proper food, and go back to the drug when they return to their homes.[10] Because of the complexities of the causal nexus and the presence of so many variables that are difficult to evaluate or isolate, it is premature to assert that coca produces poor health or intellectual deterioration. Chronic coca consumption has not been correlated with any serious long-term disease in the way cigarette smoking has been connected with heart disease and cancer. According to the United Nations Commission Report, local physicians in Peru and Bolivia say that coca users have no more cardiovascular illness than the rest of the population. The differences on intelligence tests discovered by Negrete and Murphy, which are probably similar to differences correlated with alcohol consumption, do not represent an unambiguous causal relation. Without any suggestion of a mechanism that can be experimentally established, there is simply not enough evidence that the use of coca is a cause rather than an effect of the minor evils associated with it.*

Benefits were once claimed for the use of coca in the thin air and cold of high altitudes, especially by Carlos Monge and his colleagues at the Institute for Andean Biology. Joel M. Hanna has recently revived some of these claims in a modified form. He emphasizes especially the advantage of increased heat retention through peripheral vasoconstriction and asserts that coca is not used for work at low altitudes because there heat retention is a disadvantage. But reports from the Amazon basin belie his contention that coca is not used for work in hot regions. In any case, Gutiérrez-Noriega has given convincing reasons for believing that any benefits conferred by high-altitude life on coca and vice versa are not very significant. He points out that in the time of the Incas most of the population did not use coca and that even today Indian women, whites, and *mestizos* manage to adapt to the conditions of the Andes without it. He notes that coca is used in the Amazon but not in sections of Ecuador, Argentina, and Chile that are at the same altitudes as the coca-chewing regions of Peru and Bolivia; and also that Tibet, where the natives show powers of endurance equal to or greater than those of the South American Indians, has no equivalent stimulant. He denies that there is any consistent rela

---

* For a profound study, at the epistemological level, of the difficulty in isolating variables for testing in retrospective research, where the phenomenon under examination has not been produced "to order" by the experimenter, see Paul Meehl, "Nuisance Variables and the Ex Post Facto Design," in *Analysis of Theories and Methods of Physics and Psychology,* ed. Michael Rodner and Steven Winokur, Minnesota Studies in the Philosophy of Science, vol. 4 (Minneapolis: University of Minnesota Press, 1970), pp. 373–402. Meehl points out that in any field where there is no accepted model or picture of the nature of cause and effect relations, it is impossible to decide rationally which variables to regard as potentially relevant to causal questions and which ones to factor out, whether by matching or by choice of sample population.

tionship between altitude and amount of coca consumed and points out that in some coastal areas settled by migrants from the mountains the coca habit remains common. What counts, he says (providing data), is not primarily altitude but the presence of coca plantations nearby—in other words, availability of the drug. Gutiérrez-Noriega also denies that coca is useful in the long run for heavy physical labor at high altitudes. Opposing the contention that the inhabitants of the Andes constitute a climatically determined racial variation with more resistance to the toxic effects of cocaine than other peoples, he asks why, in that case, Monge and others do not assume that the Indians' susceptibility to the useful stimulant effects of the drug is also reduced.[11]

Gutiérrez-Noriega admits that the respiratory stimulant and antifatigue action of coca may be useful on the heights in an emergency. In fact, amphetamines have been shown to counteract temporarily the effects of oxygen deficiency, and coca is a popular remedy for *soroche*, or altitude sickness. But, as we have noted, stimulants cannot produce energy but only regulate its employment and distribution. People who are physiologically adjusted to mountain conditions should have less rather than more need of stimulants for this kind of purpose. The adaptation of the respiratory and cardiovascular systems that acclimatizes them to low oxygen pressure should not require the complement of a drug; there is also no clear reason to believe that a stimulant harmful at sea level would be innocuous at an altitude of 10,000 feet.

Effects of Chronic Cocaine Use— Moderate Doses

If the evidence on the long-term effects of coca consumption is inconclusive, information on the effects of chronic cocaine sniffing or injection in small or moderate doses is even more sparse and entirely anecdotal. The works on cocainism * by Maier and by Joël and Fränkel concentrate on a condition parallel to alcoholism in which the drug has damaged its user's health and disrupted his life. No one has systematically studied the kind of cocaine use that is analogous to social drinking and is connected with serious abuse along the same kind of con-

---

* This is a term it might be useful to revive, along with morphinism, heroinism, barbituratism, caffeinism, nicotinism, and so on. By designating other forms of drug abuse with terms parallel to alcoholism, we would be emphasizing that they are neither necessarily worse nor essentially different.

tinuum that joins social drinking with alcoholism. We have already discussed the desired effects of "social snorting." The main undesirable effects, aside from financial depletion, are of several kinds: nervousness, irritability, and restlessness from overstimulation, sometimes extending to mild paranoia; physical exhaustion and mental confusion from insomnia; undesired weight loss; fatigue or lassitude in coming down; and various afflictions of the nasal mucous membranes and cartilage. Just as occasional headache, nausea, hangover, or embarrassing behavior is not enough to prevent people from drinking alcohol, so users of cocaine do not regard the evils we have just described as serious enough to outweigh its virtues. Although Maier designates the habit of using the drug in this intermittent fashion with the formidable appellation "periodic endogenous cocaine addiction" (*Kokainsucht*—*Sucht* means literally "craze" or "mania"), he states that it causes no lasting psychological or physical harm and is not a serious illness. Joël and Fränkel refer to a "symptomless, safe-appearing picture" in cocaine sniffing that may be misleading.[12]

There is very little to be said about this in any systematic way. As a matter of taste and temperament, some people do not enjoy cocaine, as some do not like alcohol. One man we interviewed said, "I didn't like the way it affected my friends, the way the people around me acted when they snorted it. . . . If I had snorted coke . . . I would think about what I had to do ahead of time, rather than let it come naturally. . . . It hardly seems as though anybody really happy . . . is involved with cocaine, that I know." Another said, "Most of the people who are heavily into coke, coke freaks, the coke scene, I don't like . . . heavy-duty macho craziness." There were complaints of a hollow feeling that demands more and more of the drug, jitteriness, being "strung out," and later, fatigue: "It's too jittery. If you do a whole lot of it, you get sort of zombied out and you tend to stare at things." (A "whole lot" meant about five grams sniffed.) Others dislike the effect on their nasal and oral membranes. The rock musician Paul Kantner has been quoted as saying (in 1972), "I stopped using coke a year and a half ago, when it was obvious it had become more dangerous than useful to me. . . . You can function and work relatively clearly on it, like for 12 or 15 hours straight. . . . But it's not controllable. . . . And when you're heavily into it, it makes you cold to people. Also it can get you physically fucked up [he is referring to the nasal passages]."[13] A woman we had previously interviewed wrote this account for us of the misgivings that eventually caused her to cut down her consumption of cocaine and then give it up except for rare occasions:

Once I started having my own coke around, it was easy to snort more and more of it. What had been a once-a-week treat became almost a daily necessity. Because coke made me feel better—more on top of things and able to pay strict attention to the longest work projects—I did not heed what I considered to be the negative aspects: the amount of money I was putting into a drug, the colds and dripping nose that inevitably followed a lot of use, the number of cigarettes I enjoyed smoking after using a lot of coke, and the frazzled efforts to come down and sleep after a day of work and drugs. I could tell I was abusing myself physically by doing all the coke I was doing. . . . My involvement with work and drugs allowed me to get by thinking about me, which meant thinking about being alone and depressed. It got to be that I didn't want to come down. . . .

I became worried about seeing shadows flitting by in the corner of my vision. It was harder to control my feelings of urgency about getting some work done or seeing to a request by someone at the station. I experienced a constant sense of something pressing on me, urging me to work faster, live faster. . . . I needed to use more depressants—alcohol, Librium, and sleeping pills—to cool myself out. Talking to other people when I was on coke became difficult. I didn't have time for it, or I found the effort to concentrate on what they were saying too difficult. I had noticed other people experiencing similar reactions. . . .

I wonder what role cocaine played in unearthing parts of me that had previously been inaccessible. Sometimes I see it as beneficial. And at other times I see it as having scattered parts of me all over the place. Parts of me that I must now work hard to make sense of and live with. So my feelings about cocaine are mixed. I fear it and am somewhat excited and attracted to it. I don't like the way it contributed to my refusing to see the consequences of the way I was living. I don't like the way it tempted me to ignore my physical and mental well-being. And I see this in other people who love coke.

Most, but not all, people who begin to feel the way this woman did apparently find it possible to do what she did.

More commonly, even people who had experienced some of the undesirable consequences of chronic use and were wary of cocaine, especially in large amounts, told us that they would probably use more if they could afford it. Some who are already using a large amount will occasionally just leave it alone for a while. The cocaine dealer "Jimmy" told Richard Woodley that if he put his finger in his nose and drew blood, or found himself becoming too hot-tempered, or his speech becoming slurred, he would stop using the drug for a day or two. Every once in a while he would stop for a longer time to "clean my system and heal my nose up." He also had to cope with fatigue from lack of sleep.[14] Some people find that these inconveniences make cocaine unappealing to them and others do not.

Aleister Crowley was a British poet, novelist, literary eccentric, cult leader, and drug and sex experimenter of the early twentieth century. In diaries, memoirs, novels, and pamphlets he left a record of the effects of cocaine and other drugs on him over a period of more than two decades. His writings are especially interesting because they illustrate the great variations in attitude one habitual user can feel. In a pamphlet he wrote in 1917 in opposition to the Harrison Act and the outlawing of cocaine, he described the drug as safe for a wise man but not for a fool. The happiness it produced, he wrote, was not passive and placid (he may have been contrasting it with opiates) but self-conscious. He also described, apparently not from his own experience, the hallucinations (including insects under the skin) and senseless craving that could accompany severe abuse. He opposed legislation against cocaine and suggested that the "drug fiend" who abused it would serve as a warning to his neighbors.[15]

At that time Crowley was certain that he and not cocaine was the master. Later he became less sure that he or anyone else could use it wisely. In his *Confessions* he recounted the case of a woman friend who took up to one-fourth ounce (about seven grams) of cocaine a day and had to switch to morphine and then alcohol in order not to destroy herself. He wrote, "I admire her . . . for her superb courage in curing herself." Despite his apprehensions, Crowley continued to use the drug: at one point in his life he was sniffing heroin continually and also indulging in three or four bouts of cocaine a week.[16]

Crowley's diaries of 1914 to 1920 show the ambivalence most clearly. He describes the cocaine effect: "The first dose produces a curiously keen delight, rather formless. . . . There's a memory-throb and a promise of new life. The next dose or two creates a curious nervousness. . . . It reminds one of the timidity of a boy before seduction. . . . This state is succeeded by a kind of anxiety and restlessness, not unlike that of a man who means to spend the evening in some kind of amusement, can't make up his mind what to do, and is irritable at his own indecision. . . . I flutter about, I toy with things. . . . The next stage is that I am aware of the master in the saddle. . . . We are off, a long, level, easy gallop, every muscle glowing with delight, the lungs intoxicated with deep draughts of pure sweet air, the heart strong and the brain clear. I am intensely happy, utterly calm, wholly concentrated." But "With big doses . . . the mind seems paralyzed; I am nailed to two or three thoughts, usually quite meaningless. . . . I notice how my mind's reaction to the experiment is always fear-laden," much more than with other drugs (apparently a mild paranoid reaction); and "the next day, even after a long night's rest, is likely to find me dull, bored, heavy," a weariness from which more cocaine provides a tempting release. At times, "I've had about a gramme and I feel nothing but a sort of nervousness." After a while, "I am now bored by the experiment . . . cocaine results are monotonous." Eventually he is writing that "cocaine's pleasure is not worth the candle." [17]

The alternation of praise and derogation in Crowley's writings is particularly interesting because he apparently had not experienced the more lurid symptoms of severe cocaine abuse that we have mentioned and will discuss in more detail. In 1922, shortly after the period when the diary entries we have quoted were written, he wrote and published an autobiographical novel, *Diary of a Drug Fiend*, in which his inner debate continues. By this time Crowley had begun to use heroin, prescribed by a physician for asthma, and at the start of 1922 he was abusing both drugs and suffered from itching, vomiting, insomnia, diarrhea, and restlessness (which sound like cocaine effects or heroin abstinence symptoms). Still he favored the free sale and use of psychoactive drugs and denied that a "drug habit" existed.[18]

In the novel itself cocaine sets off a romance, as it stimulates the hero sexually and makes him feel himself "any man's master." He is "like a choking man . . . released at the last moment, filling his lungs for the first time with oxygen." The effects on his beloved are similarly exhilarating, and marriage and a honeymoon with plenty of cocaine and extravagant descriptions of rapture follow. Physical pleasures are "etherealized"; the stimulation of cocaine is "calm and profound," not coarse like that of alcohol; it produces "ecstatic excitement and inextinguishable laughter." But disillusionment begins to set in. "Cocaine is merely Dutch courage." It destroys one's power of calculation and cannot be taken in moderation. Man and wife now start sniffing heroin "when the cocaine showed any signs of taking the bit in its teeth." The woman writes in her fictional diary: "I can't think about anything except getting H. I don't seem to mind so much about C. I never liked C much. It made me dizzy and ill." And later, "I wonder whether it's H or C or mixing the two that's messing up my mind." But when cocaine becomes available again, she writes, "And I thought I didn't like it! It's the finest stuff there is." But again, when the cocaine is gone, Crowley's hero calls it "no good without the H." He emphasizes the difference between the physical craving for heroin and the "moral" pull of cocaine. Each time he is able to get more cocaine he feels "recovered divinity" and self-confidence.

Eventually he becomes involved in a scheme to sell the drug, and his ambivalence reaches great intensity: "On the one side I was exuberantly delighted to find myself in possession of boundless supplies of cocaine; on the other I was enraged with mankind for having invented the substance that had ruined my life, and I wanted to take revenge on it by poisoning as many people as I could." His wife objects to his going into business with a "murderous villain" and calls his cocaine sniffing "a vice pure and simple." Her own craving for heroin she regards as a physical disease and not a moral failing. After some guidance from a guru figure modeled on Crowley himself, the hero ends up confident that he can use cocaine "as a fencing-master uses a rapier, as an expert, without danger of wounding himself." He concludes that psychoactive drugs are "potent and dangerous expedients for increasing your natural powers" and that "the taking of a drug should be a carefully thought out and purposefully religious act." [19] Crowley ultimately gave cocaine credit for helping his writing (including *Diary of a Drug Fiend*) and some of what he called his "magickal rituals," which included copulation. But he eventually transcended his desire for large amounts of the drug, while taking heroin on prescription for the last 15 years of his life.[20]

Rhinitis

This is the most common physiological problem experienced by steady users who do not take large overdoses. Some cocaine users think the sugar and other substances used to cut the drug in the illicit trade, or a residue of hydrochloric acid from insufficient washing in the last stage of production of the hydrochloride salt, cause this affliction. Joël and Fränkel suggest that it may be partly a mechanical effect of continual sniffing on an anesthetized mucous membrane.[21] But it seems to be mainly a consequence of sympathomimetic constriction of blood vessels in the nose by particles of cocaine that lodge there. This eventually produces necrosis of the nasal tissue from lack of blood and sometimes reactive hyperemia, or congestion. In extreme cases there may be perforation of the cartilaginous part of the septum, the wall between the nostrils; but this seems to be rare today. Bacterial infections also occur. The most common symptoms are runny, clogged, inflamed, swollen, or ulcerated noses which may be painfully sensitive and frequently bleed.

A Russian physician, Leon Natanson, examined 98 heavy cocaine users (1.5 to 10 grams a day) in a hospital for venereal disease and a clinic in Moscow in 1920. Ninety-four had nasal lesions, and 89 had perforated septa. He discounted syphilis as a cause, because the lesions appeared only in the cartilage and because only cocaine-using syphilitics had them. Reviewing the literature in 1936, Natanson noted that another physician had examined 32 upper-class cocaine users; 10 had perforations of the septum and 10 others had ulcerations. In an experimental study on animals with cocaine vapor administered through the nose, another researcher had noticed no nasal effects; but Natanson concluded that the doses he used were not high enough.[22]

The nasal syndrome was so common in Germany in the 1920s that cocaine users had a slang name for it: *Koksnase*. It is so common today that, according to one of our interview subjects, "People on the air who sound obviously stuffed up will say to the audience, 'Gee, I have this terrible cold'; it's a big in-joke." Several people we interviewed reported nosebleed, sores, runny noses, or sneezing fits that would go away if they stopped using cocaine for a while. Joël and Fränkel mention that in some of their patients the bridge of the nose was sunken in the cartilaginous part.[23] Because of its sympathomimetic effect, cocaine at first stimulates respiration and dries the nasal mucosa; so it was once used, like amphetamines, for hay fever, asthma, and colds (by Crowley, for example) in spite of warnings that the temporary relief would give way to rebound congestion and rhinitis. Today some cocaine users carry a container of nasal spray decongestant like phenylephrine with them to counter these effects, or rinse the nasal passage with warm water after sniffing. Others recommend taking care in sniffing to prevent degeneration of the cartilage, if nothing else, by allowing the drug to touch only the upper, bony part of the septum.

Effects of Chronic Cocaine Use— Large Doses

Literary descriptions based on observation convey some feeling of the consequences of a damaging cocaine habit. The condition of cocaine abusers among the Paris demimonde after World War I is described in several passages of the novel *Cocaine*, written by an Italian journalist, Dino Segré, under the pen name of Pitigrilli and first published in 1921. In spite of its decayed romanticism and melodramatic mannerisms, Segré's novel is useful because it shows evidence of firsthand familiarity with the situation it describes. In it a warning is delivered to a young man by his slightly older mistress: "You're still in time. . . . I know the workings of that dreadful and deadly powder. You have not yet reached the stage of frightful depressions, the period of brooding and destructive melancholy. You can still smile, though your blood be filled with venom. You are in the first stages yet, when one again becomes a mere boy." Restless craving is described: " 'My nights,' they will tell you, 'are agitated by dreadful shivering; insomnia tortures me; it is atrocious to be without the drug, but the thought of not knowing where to get it is even more atrocious.' " "The hands of cocaine-addicts," Segré writes, "seem always to be on the verge of some convulsion which is held in check with tremendous difficulty. . . . Their nostrils become monstrously dilated to catch imaginary particles of cocaine hovering in mid-air." At the last stage they plunge, "brain reeling in a veil of thick gloom, into utter degradation, down, down through the pit and toward final misery." Cocaine is an ambivalent symbol in the book: the hero addresses his dazzling mistress by the name of the drug, and it also serves as "a symbol of the death to which we all succumb . . . the fierce and subtle and sweet death—truly, a thing of black shadows, like some nameless cataclysm, which we inflict upon ourselves voluntarily." [24] A few of the phenomena described here, especially "dreadful shivering," sound more like results of opiate addiction, and might be discounted as a case of mistaken identity. But Segré elsewhere describes accurately the exhilarating immediate effect of cocaine and convincingly portrays the scenes where it is used. Even if only a small minority of cocaine users are ever reduced to this condition, it remains a possibility.

Vladimir Nabokov portrays a cocaine abuser in a short story written in 1924:

Too-frequent sniffs of cocaine had ravaged his mind; the little sores on the inside of his nostrils were eating into the septum. . . . During the leisure hours when the crystal-bright waves of the drug beat at him, penetrating his thoughts with their radiance and transforming the least trifle into an ethereal miracle, he painstakingly noted on a sheet of paper all the various steps he intended to take in order to trace his wife. As he scribbled, with all those sensations still blissfully taut, his jottings seemed exceedingly important and correct to him. In the morning, however, when his head ached and his shirt felt clammy and sticky, he looked with bored disgust at the jerky, blurry lines. Recently, though, another idea had begun to occupy his thoughts . . . his life had wasted away to nothing and there was no use continuing it. . . .

He kept licking his lips and sniffling . . . suddenly he could stand it no longer. . . . He locked himself in the toilet. Carefully calculating the jolts of the train, he poured a small mound of the powder on his thumbnail; greedily applied it to one nostril, then to the other; inhaled; with a flip of his tongue licked the sparkling dust off his nail; blinked hard a couple of times from the rubbery bitterness, and left the toilet, boozy and buoyant, his head filling with icy delicious air . . . he thought: how simple it would be to die right now! He smiled. He had best wait till nightfall. It would be a pity to cut short the effect of the enchanting poison.[25]

Maier lists the symptoms of chronic cocaine abuse in more clinical language as nervous excitability, anxiety, hypersensitivity to noises, flight of ideas, graphomania (compulsive scribbling), memory disturbances, mood swings, feebleness, senile appearance, emaciation, heightened reflexes with muscular unrest, fast pulse, impotence, insomnia. There is also a syndrome he calls "cocaine insanity" that sometimes arises after chronic abuse: optical and auditory hallucinations, delusions of persecution and grandeur, jealousy, violent tendencies—often with clear consciousness and insight on the part of the abuser. In this condition minor frustrations may cause energetic suicide attempts. In the late stages of chronic cocaine intoxication, there may be spontaneous abortion, twitches, cold extremities, and even paralysis.[26]

Maier also describes in some detail the hallucinations or perceptual distortions induced by an excess of cocaine. They are usually related to increased perceptual sensitivity and derived from external stimuli that are objectively observable. They may be overpowering even when the victim recognizes them for what they are; one patient heard the voice of a friend in a distant city saying that she needed his help, and, knowing that it was a hallucination, still boarded a train and traveled to that city. Perceptual distortions include faraway voices sounding near at hand, inanimate objects taking on physiognomies, "electricity" flowing through the fingers, random street noises organized into the sound of marching feet, and so on. There may be distortions of the kinesthetic sense including feelings of lightness, flying, or lengthened extremities, and even a sensation of having left one's body. Sniffers, according to Maier, usually suffer only auditory and visual hallucinations. Injectors more often have tactile hallucinations, especially the sensation of small animals under the skin, also known as "coke bugs"; this may be associated with larger quantities of the drug or faster entry into the bloodstream. Maier points out, incidentally, that the victim remains temporally and spatially well oriented and that most cocaine abusers never have hallucinations at all.[27]

How to classify the distorted or anomalous perceptual states induced by stimulants is a diagnostic and terminological problem related to the general inadequacy of our categories for describing all such conditions. It is always difficult to define degrees of perceived reality and implied deleteriousness. Without going into these questions, we can note some comparisons between the hallucinations and delusions in cocaine abuse and those of alcoholism. With cocaine the ego attends to the ordinary environment along with the distortions and delusions more than with alcohol. The visual hallucinations are usually brighter, more colorful, and more closely related to the mind's normal feeling-complex. Motor disturbances (except punding) and giddiness are much rarer than in alcoholism. Joël and Fränkel point out that the cocaine abuser may want to go on taking the drug even though, with the typical clear consciousness, he *knows* that it is making him paranoid. The accompanying self-magnification is too enjoyable.[28]

In Maier's experience, the delusions that sometimes accompany cocaine abuse may lack the association disturbances, blockages, and seemingly senseless outbreaks of emotion and leaps of thought characteristic of schizophrenia, but otherwise they resemble paranoid states. Joël and Fränkel judge that the most common psychological effect of acute and chronic overdose is irrational fear of burglars, policemen, or other enemy strangers. A cocaine abuser may sit in front of his door holding a revolver for hours, lying in wait for an imaginary intruder. Lawrence Kolb mentions a man who "used a hatchet to attack a laundry bag in his bathroom because he believed it contained a policeman." Maier notes that delusions of grandeur may be related to occupation: the physician thinks he has found a cancer cure, the engineer believes he has invented a perpetual motion machine, the soldier in wartime imagines he has discovered a new weapon or an infallible military strategy. This kind of delusion is an exaggeration of the questionable self-confidence and sense of mastery induced by stimulants; Maier notes that the confidence with which cocaine abusers express their delusory ideas has great suggestive power, especially over wives and girl friends.

A common element in the delusions and hallucinations experienced by the cocaine abuser is the tendency toward an exaggerated sense of meaningfulness, especially of environmental details. It often results in a need to *order* things that first shows itself in phenomena like a compelling desire to pull a glass back from the edge of a table, senseless counting, picture hanging, or avoidance of sidewalk cracks, and a sudden anxious need to look for some object systematically even thought it is in sight. Joël and Fränkel assert that this last condition was so common that it had a slang name among German cocaine users: *Suchkokolores*.[29] The need to put everything in order may be related both to the obsessive repetitious stereotyped activity known as punding and to the paranoid delusions that objectify and organize intellectually the anxiety produced by an excess of cocaine. According to Joël and Fränkel, some of their patients regarded

grimaces and chewing movements as distinguishing signs of heavy cocaine use. Intravenous cocaine in dogs administered for a long time eventually produces the same kind of head weaving, chop licking, and jaw
snapping as amphetamines. Joël and Fränkel note a direct transition in
their patients from senseless writing, counting, teeth grinding, and pac-
ing to full-scale paranoia. The condition observed by Ellinwood in his
study of amphetamine psychosis seems to apply to cocaine as well: "emotional enhancement of certain forms of thinking, examining, attention to
details and significance, interacting with certain forms of hyperactive peripheral attention, suspiciousness, and fear . . . to produce paranoid de-
lusional systems." [30]

As a further introduction to this topic, here is an esthetically elaborated
fictional case study by William Burroughs, whom we have already quoted
on "popping coke in the mainline":

> One morning you wake up and take a speedball [heroin or morphine and
> cocaine], and feel bugs under your skin. 1890 cops with black mustaches
> block the doors and lean in through the windows snarling their lips back from
> blue and gold embossed badges. Junkies march through the rooms singing the
> Moslem Funeral Song, bear the body of Bill Gains, stigmata of his needle
> wounds glow with a soft blue flame. Purposeful schizophrenic detectives sniff
> at your chamber pot. It's the coke horrors. . . . Sit back and play it cool and
> shoot in plenty of that GI M [morphine].

Burroughs also reports on coke horrors from sniffing: "I knew this cop in
Chicago sniff coke used to come in form of crystals, blue crystals. So he
go nuts and start screaming the Federals is after him and run down this
alley and stick his head in the garbage can. And I said, 'What you think
you are doing?' and he say, 'Get away or I shoot you. I got myself hid
good.' " [31] Making allowances for the exaggeration in Burroughs' comic-
terrifying literary manner, we can say that he hits off very well many of
the psychological themes in extreme stimulant abuse: tactile and other
hallucinations, paranoia, the use of depressant drugs to calm down.

The reported cases of psychosis and other ill effects are mostly from the
period 1885–1930, when cocaine abuse was more common than it is
today and cocaine abusers came to doctors' offices more often. Maier
claimed to have studied 100 cocaine psychoses in Zurich in the early
1920s, aside from his cases of "chronic cocainism." He includes in his
book 35 case histories—28 men and 7 women—of acute and (mainly)
chronic cocaine intoxication. Of these, 18 managed to achieve enduring
abstinence from the drug, 5 relapsed, 4 killed themselves, and the fate of
the rest was not known. Twenty-nine of the 35 were between 17 and 30

years old, but 4 of them were physicians in their 40s. Occupations and social status varied, but most were professionals or other members of the middle class.[32]

Five of the cases exemplify what Maier calls cocaine addiction (*Kokainsucht*). Their symptoms were troublesome but not severe, little more than exaggerations of the inconveniences most social users of cocaine tolerate. One man said that the only ill effect he noticed was a feeling of great fatigue on coming home from work that he knew could be relieved by more cocaine. He regarded this as a warning signal and simply stopped using the drug. A law student experienced perceptual sharpening and distortions while using cocaine. Another man, who had never sniffed more than 1.5 grams a day or on two successive days, had sexual fantasies of beautiful women, then homosexual fantasies in which he imagined himself a woman, and eventually sadistic and masochistic fantasies. A woman who sniffed 4 to 5 grams a day became sleepless and lost her appetite. Her weight fell by 10 kg and acquaintances noticed that she was alternately lively and anxiously dreamy. She, like the other cases of *Kokainsucht*, gave up the drug without much difficulty.[33]

Maier discusses his largest group of patients under the heading "chronic cocainism." Four of the twelve recovered, one committed suicide with barbiturates, four relapsed, and the fate of the others was unknown. In this condition alternating states of exaltation and depression were common, even when there was no psychosis or delirium. Loss of sexual feeling was universal. One man remembered hunting through a house at night for nonexistent mice with his friends and at another time asking a chambermaid why the hotel orchestra was playing until dawn. Another would go on a cocaine bender or run for two weeks and then lie in bed for three days, "sweating frightfully." In still another case, a man started by sniffing one gram of cocaine on Saturdays and found that it excited him sexually and did no apparent harm. As he raised the dose and took the drug more often, up to four grams in a night, depression and self-reproaches began whenever he abstained. He lost all sexual interest and began to feel spiders crawling on his skin. When he had taken a great deal of cocaine he felt an urge to drink alcohol and smoke tobacco. At the time he was examined he was pale and thin, and had difficulty getting up in the morning. He lacked energy and felt apathetic. He often thought that people on the street were staring at him or detectives following him.

In another case a 19-year-old student came to Maier because he was nervous and his physical and mental faculties were declining. He had been sniffing four to five grams a day and was stealing to get money to buy the drug. He would often fall asleep in class if he did not have it. His symptoms included tactile hallucinations, pounding of the heart, and a tendency to mechanical repetitive movements. He had no sexual feelings but saw images of beautiful women in the clouds and spoke to them. Once he started writing or talking he could not stop. Sleep was unpleasantly heavy and dreamless. During cocaine intoxication colors were brighter and more beautiful, small sounds seemed loud, he heard whole symphonies when clocks struck, he felt able to solve all problems but thought it unnecessary to do so. During abstinence, on the other hand, every prospect was displeasing and man too was vile. Eventually he stopped taking cocaine, but Maier is not sure whether he kept his resolution to "cure myself entirely." [34]

Maier also discusses something he calls subacute cocaine delirium, which tends to arise after cocainism is well established and lasts a few hours to a few days. The fictional cases described by Burroughs would probably fall into this category. Maier divides these cases, some of which also might be called cocaine psychoses, into three types: euphoric with delusions of grandeur; paranoid-anxious; and dreamy-passive with cinematographic images. Of course, there are also various combinations of the three. We have already discussed many of the symptoms. In one case a man thought his boss was hiring journalists to put allusions to him in the newspapers and paying actors to blow their noses conspicuously in public places in reference to his habit. There were other, less amusing kinds of paranoia. For example, a young man began to think that his father, from whom he had been stealing, was sending men to persecute him; he threatened these imaginary persecutors with weapons.[35]

We have already described the symptoms of what Maier calls cocaine insanity, a more prolonged and systematized version of subacute delirium. Maier discusses four cases, including two physicians who were what he calls morphiococainists, injecting both drugs intravenously. In one case the physician took morphine for headaches, then used cocaine to reduce the pain of the injections. The combination caused hyperexcitation, shortness of breath, and anxiety. His wife also took cocaine, and both of them then used scopolamine to calm down. The wife took an overdose of this drug and died. He began to have visual hallucinations, said he had to follow his wife, and believed electric currents were running through his body, that he was about to die, and that he could hear people plotting against him. Even before he reached this condition, as he took less and less morphine and finally cocaine alone, he had suffered hallucinations, jealous delusions, and torturing anxiety, and his career had fallen into ruins. Eventually he gave up cocaine and was cured.

In an even more serious case, a physician was given cocaine to increase his energy during an attempted withdrawal from morphine. He began to occupy himself with delusionary research projects, thinking that he had found new cures for astigmatism and cataracts, and that spectacles should be made out of protein because glass tended to concentrate the effects of an invisible destructive ray. He wandered about the house at night and heard imaginary burglars. At times he believed he had a cancer cure or a new theory of colors. Eventually his colleagues brought him to Maier's clinic because they thought he might harm a patient. Upon arrival his condition was described as euphoria with flight of ideas. He had microscopic hallucinations and expressed sexual fantasies. He did not speak willingly of his discoveries because he knew that others thought him mad. By that time he was injecting five or six grams of cocaine a day and about 300 mg of morphine. His morphine and cocaine were taken away, but eventually he went back to them and died of arteriosclerosis combined with an overdose of one or another or both of the drugs.[36] A similar case was reported in 1886 by D. R. Brower: a physician who injected up to a gram a day of cocaine intravenously and suffered from pallor, emaciation, and insomnia, became irritable, believed he had a mission to give everyone the drug, carried a pistol and threatened vengeance on doubters, neglected his practice and alienated his friends, and fell into poverty.[37]

The self-description of a physician who was a cocaine abuser, published in 1920, sums up many of the phenomena we have been discussing. "Dr. Schlwa" first took morphine in 1916. In October 1917 he began to use cocaine to aid withdrawal. As he raised the dose, signs of psychosis appeared and he quit both drugs. But in November 1918, at a moment of deep depression and nervous exhaustion, he began to take morphine and then cocaine again. He came to a clinic sleepless, talking cheerfully with an edge of anxiety, and complaining of "worms" in his body and "animals" in his room which he knew were hallucinations. He spoke of a fear of burglars which was beginning to turn into a systematic persecutory delusion. After injecting 50 to 200 mg of cocaine subcutaneously, he said, he felt euphoria, a fast pulse, and slow deep breathing, with a desire to talk and run. After a half hour there was less euphoria and more nervousness, and a desire for more cocaine—with morphine to reduce the anxiety.

After three weeks of one gram of cocaine a day, 100 to 200 mg subcutaneously produced painful, deep, slow breathing, fast light pulse, and cold extremities. The effect was now more paralytic than excitant. The hallucinations started to take control. Taking 400 mg of cocaine and 600 mg of morphine subcutaneously, he felt orgasmic euphoria. In the later stages of chronic intoxication the cocaine effects dominated those of morphine. A little of either drug would eliminate first his potency and then his sexual desire. He regarded the feeling of mental activity under the influence of cocaine as "bustling without depth" that left nothing of value behind. Sleep was dreamless. The stages of euphoria, psychosis, and paralysis were sharply separated.[38]

It is not clear why some cocaine users succumb to chronic abuse and psychosis when most do not. We can hardly expect to be able to answer this question adequately for cocaine when it has so far proved unanswerable in the much more numerous and better studied cases of alcohol, amphetamines, and opiates. There may be a personality type predisposed to the abuse of some particular drug or of drugs in general, but no one has been able to define that personality type for any practical purpose like diagnosis and prevention. The questionable research technique that finds "personality defects" and "pathology" *post factum* in people who have either actually harmed themselves or others with drugs or gotten into trouble with the law by using drugs (like marihuana) that have failed to receive respectable society's capriciously granted seal of approval is not only delusively easy to use by stretching definitions but often hypocritical and otherwise morally odious. (We will have more to say about this when we discuss the subject of drug dependence in Chapter 8). Maier does not presume to find any common pattern in the life histories of his cocaine abusers.

The most we can say is that in all probability whatever conditions are apt to produce amphetamine psychosis and amphetamine abuse are also apt to produce cocaine psychosis and cocaine abuse. The 50-year-old reports on symptoms of cocaine abuse bear an uncanny resemblance to more recent descriptions of amphetamine abuse. The Swedish physician Nils Bejerot has been impelled to write (his italics): *"the well-established amphetamine-Preludine-Ritaline-toxicomanias in all essentials resemble cocainism."* [39] He makes a good case for his assertion. But cocaine, as it is habitually used today, does not produce these symptoms nearly so often as amphetamines, partly because of a difference in pharmacological properties and partly because the illegality and exorbitant price of cocaine make it hard to obtain large quantities.

Because of this resemblance, it is useful to consider what is known about amphetamine psychosis. In some cases amphetamine only precipitates schizophrenia in an ambulatory schizophrenic or preschizophrenic who has been using it because it seems to combat the incipient symptoms of the disease. But amphetamine abusers may also be wrongly diagnosed as preschizophrenic or schizophrenic on the basis of symptoms actually caused by the drug. O. J. Kalant, for example, believes that in 109 of 201 cases of psychotic reactions associated with amphetamines that she studied, the drug alone was responsible. Psychosis occurs most commonly when a chronic abuser takes a larger amount than usual in a short period of time. Many cases of amphetamine psychosis are probably unreported or misdiagnosed as toxic psychoses caused by other drugs or as paranoid schizophrenia. The condition is often distinguishable from the latter only by blood tests for drugs or its short duration—only a few days or perhaps weeks after the drug is withdrawn. It is sometimes asserted, however, that a predominance of visual hallucinations, relatively appropriate affect, and a setting of clear consciousness, correct spatiotemporal orientation, and hyperacute memory of the psychotic episode distinguish amphetamine psychosis from schizophrenia. In assessing the incidence of amphetamine psychosis it is important to note that amphetamine abusers may live among fellow "speed freaks" who tolerate their paranoid symptoms, or they may learn to discount the paranoia as an effect of the drug.[40] Although cocaine may not be so fertile as amphetamines in producing either chronic drug abuse or psychosis, most of the symptoms and conditions, including the high incidence of misdiagnosed and unreported cases, are probably similar.

It is doubtful whether cocaine ever causes a chronic psychosis, i.e., one that persists long after the drug is withdrawn. Heilbronner studied this question as early as 1913 and concluded that there was no typical chronic cocaine psychosis and that the apparent examples were only cases in which cocaine-induced symptoms "colored" an endogenous psychosis. Maier agreed with Heilbronner and stated that any paranoid condition remaining a few months after the cessation of cocaine abuse was probably schizophrenia. The analogy with amphetamines may again help us here. Although chronic amphetamine intoxication may have some role in producing a longer-lasting disturbance, it is not easy to distinguish this effect, if it exists, from endogenous or reactive schizophrenia.[41]

Gutiérrez-Noriega has produced an inhibition of the central nervous system resembling catatonia experimentally in dogs by the continued administration of large doses of cocaine. He injected 5 mg per kg per day intravenously into 13 dogs and 10 mg per kg per day into 2 others, for a period of one to three years (the equivalent of 350 mg and 700 mg in a 150-pound man). Five of the animals began to adopt cataleptic postures with waxy flexibility (preservation of abnormal limb positions) for several hours after injections, and showed either motor inhibition or alternating states of inhibition and excitation. They also exhibited stereotyped movements, sometimes so complex that they looked like a ritual dance. During the cataleptic states, symptoms of parasympathetic excitation like bradycardia (slow heart rate) and copious flow of saliva appeared. The change from an inhibited to an excited state was often marked by piloerection (hair standing on end), a sign of strong sympathetic nervous system arousal. In the cataleptic states, they were insensible to pain—an analgesia deeper than that produced by barbiturate narcosis or general anesthesia. Barbiturates suppressed the analgesia and all the catatonic manifestations, both excitatory and inhibitory, but actually intensified normal locomotor activity. Ephedrine and other sympathomimetic drugs intensified all the symptoms suppressed by barbiturates, including the bradycardia normally associated with parasympathetic action.[42]

Gutiérrez-Noriega and others believe that cocaine-induced inhibition of the central nervous system is an active process caused by selective arousal of inhibitory neurons (neurons that suppress further nerve activity when stimulated) and not a form of depression or narcosis. Excitatory and inhibitory neurons are closely associated in the body, and it is apparently not even clear whether epinephrine acts by arousing the former or blocking the latter. Larry Stein and G. David Wise suggest that the norepinephrine liberated by amphetamine serves largely to depress behaviorally suppressive cells in the brain, i.e., disinhibits rather than directly excites. Cocaine potentiates both excitatory and inhibitory responses to externally introduced norepinephrine in sympathetic nerves. Gutiérrez-Noriega believes that the reason why barbiturates suppress the cataleptic states induced by cocaine and produce a subsequent "noncatatonic" motor excitement may be that they have more depressant effect on inhibitory neurons than on excitatory neurons. It is as though chronic cocaine intoxication sometimes produced a condition in which inhibitory and excitatory neurons in the sympathetic system were in fierce competition for control over behavior.[43] The analogy between this condition and some of the manifestations of catatonic schizophrenia in human beings is striking; cocaine psychosis, like amphetamine psychosis, has been proposed as an experimental model for studying the functional psychoses that might help in determining their neurochemical mechanisms. We shall discuss this further in Chapter 7, which deals with the uses of cocaine in medicine and psychiatry.

Chronic Physiological Effects—Large Doses

The physiological effects of chronic administration of large doses of cocaine have never been studied systematically in human beings. Vervaeck refers to tachycardia, arrhythmia, syncope, and angina pectoris in chronic cocaine users. But Joël and Fränkel, as we mentioned, rarely found cardiovascular problems in cocaine sniffers. They point out that in cocaine abuse at its worst the immediate cocaine effects are less important than complications from the ensuing malnutrition, exhaustion, nervousness, and general debility, which can be very serious. The most common specific physiological symptom is the rhinitis we have discussed; bronchitis from constant irritation of the mucous membranes occurs in some heavy users; Joël and Fränkel also report a generalized loss of pain sensitivity similar to the effect produced in dogs.[44]

In animal experiments, 15 mg per kg daily subcutaneously (the equivalent of about a gram in a 150-pound man) in dogs for six weeks produced no physical ill effects. In an experiment by Gutiérrez-Noriega and Zapata Ortiz on rats, even 100 mg per kg orally produced no chronic effects, although at 200 mg per kg growth and reproduction rate were retarded, and 1.6 grams per kg caused death in a few days. The highest tolerable subcutaneous dose was 155 mg per kg daily. (Animals with more complex brains appear to be more susceptible to the drug's psychological effects and possibly to its physical effects too. If this is true, man would of course be the most susceptible species. Gutiérrez-Noriega and Zapata Ortiz estimate the resistance of a rat to cocaine to be 20 times that of a man.) In another early experiment with rats, 75 mg per kg subcutaneously every 24 to 72 hours (the equivalent of 5 grams in a 150-pound man) caused successively restlessness, muscular weakness, fast breathing, paralysis of the hind legs, twitching, convulsions, and death after 14.2 days in males and 34.8 days in females. There was an average weight loss of 7.8 percent. Although only five rats of each sex were used, the enormously greater resistance of the females can hardly have been a chance artifact. We have seen no attempt to duplicate this extraordinary (and implausible) result and no reference to it in the later literature.[45]

Other effects that have been noticed or tested are teratogenic potential (danger of producing deformed young) and liver damage. Cocaine has proved to be the least teratogenic of several drugs, including a number of opiates, in experiments on hamsters.[46] Liver abnormalities are more positively correlated with use of cocaine. Gutiérrez-Noriega, in an experiment on chronic cocaine intoxication in dogs, produced fatty degeneration, dilation of capillaries, and other forms of liver damage. He suggests that the transformation of cocaine to ecgonine releases methyl alcohol, which is known to be toxic to the liver. Vincent Marks and P. A. L. Chapple, in their study, "Hepatic Dysfunction in Heroin and Cocaine Users," found that of 89 patients at a British psychiatric hospital who took intravenous heroin and cocaine, 80 showed liver abnormalities. When they stopped using the drugs the liver returned to normal. Marks and Chapple state that liver damage is rare in amphetamine, barbiturate, and cannabis users. They postulate a direct toxic effect of heroin and cocaine in combination, although they also think contaminants in the injected solutions might be part of the problem.[47] Morphine and heroin administered to normal animals and men cause no liver damage even over a long period of time; so, unless an adulterant or hepatitis virus is the cause or there is a special effect of heroin and cocaine in combination, we must assume that cocaine is the toxic agent. The liver is presumably damaged, in a reversible process, by detoxifying large amounts of the drug in a short time.

After admitting that information on physical changes caused by chronic abuse of cocaine is sparse, Maier goes on to discuss a case cited by Eugenio Bravetta in 1922. The man in question had sniffed cocaine for a year and died of an overdose (one of the rare cases, if the account is correct, of death from sniffing). According to his wife, he had been using no other drug. His diary described the progression from euphoria to anxiety to hallucinations as his habit became worse. Autopsy showed ulceration of the nasal septum, swollen and hyperemic brain and lungs with infarctions, enlarged spleen, enlarged liver with a hard consistency, degeneration of the walls of blood vessels in the brain and thromboses and hemorrhages in the smallest of them, and fatty infiltration of nerve cells. Unfortunately, it was not clear how much of this was caused by acute poisoning and how much by chronic abuse. Maier notes that many of the symptoms, especially nerve cell degeneration, are also characteristic of acute morphine poisoning and some infectious diseases. But the hemorrhages and thromboses in the brain and lungs, he believes, were produced specifically by cocaine's constricting action on blood vessels.[48]

We can now sum up the scarce information on the physiological and psychological effects of chronic use of cocaine. There is no clear evidence linking the ordinary habitual use of coca in South America causally with any mental or physical deficiency or disease. Although *coqueros* suffer from malnutrition and its consequences more often than men who do not chew coca, the use of the drug seems more likely to be an effect than a cause of poor diet. But there is little reason to believe that if coca should be harmful at low altitudes it might be less so or even beneficial at higher ones. Sniffing (or drinking in small doses, as in Freud's case) usually produces no more serious psychological problems than irritability, nervousness, and insomnia, with occasional depression and fatigue on coming down. Physiologically, the most common problem is rhinitis. The symptoms of chronic overuse or abuse are very similar to those of amphetamine abuse, although they apparently occur more rarely with cocaine. This is apparently a pattern produced by stimulant drugs' neurophysiological mimicry of an emergency situation. In particular, the temporary psychoses in amphetamine and cocaine abuse seem to be nearly identical. Chronic intoxication may produce a paralytic or catatonialike condition. Physiologically, malnutrition, exhaustion, and general debilitation are the most common effects of severe abuse. Cardiovascular problems may or may not arise: the evidence is inconclusive. The teratogenic potential of cocaine appears to be low (possibly because it is so quickly detoxified and excreted), but there is evidence of reversible liver damage.

A Note on Cocaine and Opiates

This matter is worth discussing separately because chronic abuse of the two drugs at the same time has been common. Although otherwise dissimilar, they have a good part of their recent history in common. The law has yoked them together and doomed them to bear the same burden of public contempt and fear. Physicians and academic authorities have too often allowed this to influence them; for example, a book entitled *Drugs and Youth,* published in 1969, devotes one section to "Morphine, Heroin, and Cocaine," thus accepting legal categories rather than pharmacological ones as a basis for discussion.[49] Writers who know better perpetuate an unnecessary confusion in this way. If we want to begin to be reasonable about the real nature and dangers of psychoactive drugs, we must avoid the casual use of socially accepted misclassifications.

The association in use that causes such misclassifications, however, is (or once was) genuine. Cocaine, as we saw, began its career as a cure for morphine addiction in the 1880s, and soon the term "morphiococainism" entered the medical vocabulary. By 1913 A. Friedlander was observing that in Europe physicians rarely saw pure cocainists. Joël and Fränkel, writing in 1924, agree that until World War I most serious cocaine abusers were also morphine or heroin addicts. When both opiates and cocaine were forced underground, the association continued, although the social status of their users changed. William Burroughs wrote in 1956 that "I have never known a habitual cocaine user who was not also a morphine addict." The drug-taking habits of opiate addicts are relatively well known—at least for those addicts, probably a small minority, who come under the control of government and medical authorities. These authorities often monitor most of their activities and inspect their urine too. In a 1970 study of 422 male addicts at New York treatment facilities, John Langrod found that 66 percent of them had used cocaine, 47 percent more than six times. Proportionately more blacks were in the latter group: 54 percent, compared to 44 percent of the Puerto Ricans and 38 percent of the whites. Usually they injected it along with heroin. Ten percent had used cocaine before they took up heroin. David E. Smith and his colleagues at the Haight-Ashbury Free Medical Clinic interviewed 303 heroin addicts in 1971 and found that 10 percent of them had used cocaine moderately to heavily. In 1972 they interviewed 147 more and found that the proportion had risen to 20.7 percent. Of "new junkies" at the Haight clinic (those who began taking heroin after January 1967), only 0.5 percent used cocaine in early 1970, but 16.3 percent in the period May 1970 to July 1971. Among methadone maintenance patients 18.5 percent in a 1972 study at Philadelphia General Hospital had cocaine in their urine. At the National Institutes of Mental Health clinic at Lexington, a third of the methadone patients in a 1973 study had used cocaine at least once and about 20 percent used it often. In Great Britain 564 registered addicts were receiving cocaine in 1968 (a number that had risen from 25 in 1958 and 171 in 1963). The corresponding numbers were 2,240 for heroin and 198 for morphine. During 1967 and 1968 many doctors replaced cocaine with methamphetamine in prescriptions in the belief that it was less dangerous. Since 1968, when private practitioners were denied the right to prescribe opiates or cocaine to addicts and treatment centers were established, legal prescriptions for cocaine have stopped almost entirely.[50] The use of cocaine by opiate addicts is a very small corner of the contemporary scene anywhere in the world. The time is long past when anyone could say that he had never known a habitual cocaine user who did not also take opiates. Cocaine is now much more likely to be combined with alcohol, marihuana, or hashish for sedation.

Since at one time such a large proportion of cocaine abusers also used opiates, it has been suggested that cocaine is rarely dangerous when used alone. Freud, as we saw, insisted that cocaine had "claimed no victims of its own." In fact, many people who *inject* cocaine use opiates too, and these are the ones most likely to come to the attention of physicians. Most cocaine sniffers have little or no contact with opiates and, concomitantly, few symptoms of severe abuse. Opiates create a steady physiological need and a distinct abstinence sickness; although the desire or craving for cocaine can be very strong, it does not produce intense physiological symptoms on withdrawal and it can be more easily used intermittently. Therefore the real problem may appear to be the combination of opiates with cocaine rather than cocaine alone.

But pharmacologically it makes no sense to say that cocaine is relatively harmless unless combined with opiates. The drugs are usually complementary in their effects, and the psychological and physiological consequences of cocaine abuse can be worse than those of opiate addiction. In the 1880s Erlenmeyer said that the only thing as bad as cocaine abuse was alcoholism. (Today he would have to add at least barbiturate and amphetamine abuse.) Burroughs observes, "A morphine addict can live to be 90. . . . Their general health is excellent. . . . On the other hand, cocaine, methedrine, and all variations of the benzedrine formula are ruinous to health, even more so than alcohol." A 1914 article on "Narcotic Addiction" expresses the same opinion: "A pure cocaine addict very rarely complains of violent cramps and diarrhea upon withdrawal of the drug. On the other hand, cocaine is more destructive than the opium derivatives, and its effects upon the body appear very early compared to the physical changes observed in morphine fiends." Louis Lewin in *Phantastica* writes of the "picture of degradation worse than Hogarth" in cocaine abuse, and declares that unlike a morphine addict, the cocaine abuser cannot "mask his disorder." In an experiment performed in 1968, monkeys allowed to administer both morphine and cocaine by means of separate catheters implanted in their jugular veins used both drugs, cocaine dominating during the day and morphine at night until the animals became so disoriented that no pattern was discernible. The combination produced delirium, motor impairment, anorexia, emaciation, and death in two to four weeks. The effect was like that of cocaine alone; morphine alone in the same experiment was continued for over a year without any damage to health except infections. According to one writer, in Britain, "most heavy heroin users take grain-for-grain doses of cocaine. . . . It is possible that much of the harm attributed to heroin is in fact caused by cocaine hydrochloride." [51] The most severe symptoms of morphiococainism, except for the opiate abstinence syndrome, were always cocaine effects. Pure opiate addicts, for example, rarely suffer hallucinations, paranoia, and psychoses: as Burroughs remarks, they tend to be drearily sane.

Here is an account of his cocaine problem by a man who first sniffed heroin, then injected it intravenously, then began to use cocaine as well (legally, in Great Britain):

> I was on cocaine from then until 1964, a good solid five years. And it really ruined me; I lost job after job, and I couldn't work, and this and that, and we were on assistance, and, oh, it was great, a great performance. . . . Oh yeah, I

die for it every time I think of it. But it does me absolutely no good. I get terrible
hallucinations, I get the horrors something awful, I'll fall asleep over my work,
and I'll swear and all this. . . . I get as paranoid as you could possibly get, or at
least as possible for me to get. . . . I see secret tunnels opening in the walls
and everything else, you know, and it's really too much. And yet, if, by some
mischance, they started to give it to me here I wouldn't refuse it. . . . Oh, I
would try to rationalize it, I suppose, that I would manage it better this time or
something. But I wouldn't.

At one time this man was taking 500 mg of heroin and 500 mg of cocaine
a day intravenously. He withdrew several times from heroin, and found it
harder when he was also taking cocaine. He was addicted to heroin at the
time of the interview, in the early 1970s. According to the authors of the
book in which his case is reported, he never had any trouble earning a living for his family except during the cocaine period.[52]

In fact, one function of opiates in the combined abuse of the two drugs
has been to prevent the cocaine from ruining the user's mental or physical health. It is possible (and for the addict sometimes necessary) to
maintain oneself on opiates, but not on stimulants, at a high level intravenously. Cocaine abusers often have to turn to some sedative drug,
and morphine and heroin are among the most effective ones available.
We have already mentioned the cases cited by Aleister Crowley, including his own (although he never injected but only sniffed the drugs).
William Halsted is an even more significant example because he had
such a distinguished professional career after he rid himself of the cocaine habit and became a morphine addict. Lawrence Kolb, writing in
1962, cites the case of a physician who, after using cocaine for 6 years
and suffering 12 "fits"—apparently delirium or psychoses—turned to
morphine to counteract what he called the horrible effects of the cocaine
and continued to use morphine alone, without pleasure, for 21 years.
Burroughs sums up: "The nervousness and depression resulting from
cocaine use are not alleviated by more cocaine. They are effectively relieved by morphine. The use of cocaine by a morphine addict always leads
to larger and more frequent injections of morphine." [53]

Since opiates were a pharmacological answer to the condition of anxiety produced by cocaine, morphine addicts "cured" with the help of cocaine often went back to morphine to cure themselves of the cocaine
habit. This was one of the main sources of "morphiococainism." We have
already mentioned some cases recorded by Maier and Mayer-Gross' "Dr.
Schlwa." Magnan and Saury in 1889 described several others. In one of
them a man who used cocaine in an attempt to rid himself of a morphine
habit that was doing him little harm except for abstinence symptoms

found himself taking both drugs. After a month he was injecting one gram of cocaine a day and after two months began to have hallucinations and became hyperexcitable. He stopped using cocaine and continued with morphine for six months; these symptoms disappeared. Then he began taking cocaine again, this time up to two grams a day, and suffered tactile hallucinations, tremors, and convulsions.[54]

The acute effect of the heroin-cocaine combination taken intravenously—a speedball—is particularly interesting. It has been described this way: "Coke hit my head, a pleasant dizziness and tension, while the morphine spread through my body in relaxing waves." In an experiment on mice, cocaine but not procaine or imipramine (an antidepressant) heightened morphine analgesia.[55] Obviously, opiates and cocaine complement each other instead of canceling each other's effects: "I felt them as distinctly different highs. It wasn't as if I felt a mixture of the two," said a man we interviewed. We have mentioned that cocaine may actually increase the lethal power of heroin in the doses used by addicts. So the acute as well as the chronic effects of a combination of cocaine and heroin may be both desired and dangerous.

We must emphasize here, although we make the point more fully in another context, that nothing is unique about this combination except its peculiar social status: unusually heavy legal penalties and public disapprobation for the use of either drug. Methamphetamine and other amphetamines have often been substituted for cocaine in the speedball and may be more dangerous. Cocaine abusers sometimes use barbiturates to calm down. Although these drugs antagonize cocaine's acute toxic effects, they are themselves dangerous and addictive. Depressants that heighten each other's lethal effect, like alcohol and barbiturates or alcohol and heroin, may be the worst combination of all.

The combination of cocaine and heroin is simply the least socially respectable modification of a common American and European cultural pattern: the use of "uppers" and "downers," alternately or together, to change one's mood chemically at will. A prescription mixture of morphine and cocaine under the name of Trivalin was used in Europe in the 1920s, in much the same way that amphetamine-barbiturate combinations with names like Dexamyl and Obedrin were used in the United States in the 1950s and 1960s. In Great Britain a mixture of morphine, heroin, and cocaine with gin or brandy, known as Brompton's cocktail, is used to assuage the pain of dying cancer patients. "Its value in terminal care is unsurpassed," according to the author of a recent British book, *Intractable Pain*.[56] Opiates and cocaine do not necessarily constitute the most dangerous of the stimulant-sedative combinations, especially if the drugs are inhaled but possibly even if they are injected. Amphetamines, barbiturates, and alcohol kill more people and ruin more lives than either cocaine or heroin. Of course, that is largely because they are so much more freely available, but it is not obvious that freely available heroin and cocaine would be any worse. In fact, heroin was sold in Sweden until 1956, under its chemical name of diacetylmorphine, in several popular cough syrups, apparently without doing appreciable harm.[57] Cocaine and heroin have come to their present status by a historical anomaly that we will discuss in Chapter 10. Clearing up the confusion about these drugs requires more than an analysis, necessary as that is, of their pharmacological properties.

7

COCAINE IN MEDICINE
AND PSYCHIATRY

TODAY the range of recognized medical uses for cocaine, outside of South American folk medicine, is very narrow. But the alkaloid was once used, and coca still is used, for a much wider variety of medicinal purposes. Like opiates, alcohol, amphetamines, and other drugs affecting the central nervous system, cocaine seemed to relieve the symptoms of many otherwise very different illnesses and functional disturbances. The use of the word *panacea* has long implied scorn, but before the full development of modern medicine, with its goal of influencing the underlying causes of clearly, usually etiologically, defined diseases instead of or in addition to providing symptomatic relief, the centrally acting cure-alls were among the most important items in the pharmacopoeia. Even 40 or 50 years after the heyday of the opiate- and cocaine-containing patent medicines, the amphetamines could be introduced to physicians and the public with a proposed range of applications very similar to those of cocaine in the 1880s and permitted to run the same gradual course of disillusionment in the medical community. Of the old panaceas only morphine retains something of its former range of application, and even it is used much more sparingly and under much stricter medical supervision than it once was. But new synthetic substances like the barbiturates and tranquilizers have been found to serve some of the same purposes. Medicine continues to have its panaceas, although it is more shamefaced about them. Nevertheless, there has been a tendency over the last century to expel the use of such drugs from the category of medicine and transfer it to the categories of superstition, religion, fun, or even disease and crime. We will say more about this historical development, which has been fateful for attitudes toward cocaine, in Chapter 10.

Because a drug like cocaine can make one feel better in so many different circumstances, it is not easy to classify the therapeutic applications. An unconventional but revealing approach is to consider how South American Indians classify the uses of coca. They have been taking the drug for over a thousand years, and their tradition contains more empirical knowledge about its effects than could possibly have been accumulated in the single generation devoted to its investigation by Western medicine in the nineteenth century. Horacio Fabrega, Jr., and Peter K. Manning, in a 1973 study entitled "Health Maintenance Among Peruvian Peasants," analyzed the functions of coca and other herbal drugs in the village of Huarocondo, Peru, population 6,000, located 25 miles north of Cuzco at the altitude of 12,500 feet. Most of the people chew coca. Fabrega and Manning listed the herbs in common use and the conditions socially defined in the village as amenable to herbal treatment. Then they interviewed a sample of 40 adult males, asking whether a given herb was useful for treating a given condition. If more than 70 percent of the subjects considered an herb helpful for a given condition, it was regarded as a standard remedy. Coca in one form or another was a standard remedy for more problems than any other herb—8 out of a total of 18 listed. Not surprisingly, it was the accepted treatment for hunger (100 percent) and cold (98 percent). It was used to improve spirits (93 percent) and provide physical strength (93 percent). It was also used for two folk illnesses: *el Soka*, a condition of weakness, fatigue, and general malaise apparently resembling neurasthenia as defined by Freud and Mortimer (73 percent); and *el Fiero*, a chronic wasting illness (73 percent). Coca was also the remedy of choice for stomach upset and pains (100 percent) and for colic, or severe gastrointestinal disturbances including diarrhea, cramps, and nausea (73 percent). Other herbs were preferred for acute high fever, headache, respiratory infections, severe mental disturbances (*la Locura*), and gastrointestinal disturbances believed to be caused by emotional difficulties (*la Colerina*).[1]

Coca is also reported to be used in the form of leaf powder or tea for stomach ulcers, rheumatism, asthma, and even malaria. Coca tea is a remedy for the nausea, dizziness, and headache of *soroche* or altitude sickness, and it is routinely served to tourists arriving at hotels and inns in the high Andes. The juice from the chewed leaf may be applied to the eye to soothe irritation, or gargled for hoarseness and sore throat. Coca also contains vitamin C and some B vitamins, and it is sometimes said to be an important source of these nutrients in the Andean diet.

The therapeutic applications favored by nineteenth-century physicians for coca and cocaine were sometimes defined differently from those common in Peru. Freud's list includes "nervous stomach disorders," asthma, diseases of the vocal cords, sexual disinterest, and convalescence from typhoid fever; Mortimer's includes uremia, vomiting in pregnancy, convalescence from yellow fever, skin conditions, stimulation of uterine contractions in childbirth, and appeasing thirst in diabetes. But except for morphine addiction, alcoholism, and surgical anesthesia, nineteenth-century medicine covers largely the same ground as the Peruvian Indians. In an appendix to his book on coca, Mortimer lists the responses to letters he sent to "a selected set" of over 5,000 physicians in 1897 asking for their observations on coca. Of the 1,206 replying, 369 said that they had used coca in their own practices. (By that time doctors were suspicious of coca because they were familiar with the dangers of cocaine abuse.) Common observations were that coca increased appetite (113 of 369 responding), raised blood pressure (88), stimulated circulation (107), strengthened the heart (117), improved digestion (104), stimulated the mind (109) and the muscles (89), improved respiration (40), and served as an aphrodisiac (60). Forty-four of the 369 claimed failure to get any results. The most popular therapeutic applications were debility, exhaustion, neurasthenia, and overwork. Smaller numbers recommended coca for anemia, melancholia, bronchitis, angina pectoris, and other conditions. Only 21 physicians thought there was a dangerous tendency to form a "coca habit." [2]

To use the CNS-stimulating effect of cocaine or coca for symptoms described as neurasthenia or exhaustion often meant little more than taking the drug to forget one's troubles or make them easier to bear—functions also served at that time by opiates and later by amphetamines, barbiturates, and tranquilizers. In fact, the distinction between the use of a substance as a medicine and its use as a drug taken for fun, like the distinction between health and pleasure, is not nearly so well defined as we usually prefer to believe and often dependent mainly on social factors like the authority under which the drug is taken. In cultures where medicine has not freed itself from religion, and in cultures like nineteenth-century Europe and the United States where the categories of medicine and pleasure overlapped more obviously than they do in our society today, it was even easier to regard the euphoriant effect of centrally acting substances as medicinal—"a harmless remedy for the blues," as the